AF539805

PRODUCTION AND MARKETING OF COCONUT

By

Dr. Mabel Sulochana
Associate Professor
Deptt. of Commerce
Nesamony Memorial Christian College
Martandam
(Tamil Nadu)

&

Dr. X. Antony Thanaraj
Associate Professor
Deptt. of Commerce
Scott Christian College
Nagercoil (Tamil Nadu)
(India)

DISCOVERY PUBLISHING HOUSE PVT. LTD.
NEW DELHI—110 002

Published by:
Tilak Wasan
DISCOVERY PUBLISHING HOUSE PVT. LTD.
4831/24, Ansari Road, Prahlad Street
Darya Ganj, New Delhi-110002 (India)
Phone: +91-11-23279245, 43764432
Fax: +91-11-23253475
E-mail: parul.wasan@gmail.com
discoverypublishinghouse@gmail.com
info@discoverypublishinggroup.com
web: www.discoverypublishinggroup.com

First Edition: **2011**
ISBN: 978-81-8356-864-7

Production and Marketing of Coconut

Printed at:
Shree Balaji Art Press
Delhi

Preface

Agriculture is playing a predominant role in the economic development of all developed and developing countries. Even since India's independence agriculture in India has taken great strides, owing to the varietal and agronomic interventions of agricultural research and the resourcefulness of the farming community.

Coconut is unique among the horticulture crops, raised in India because of the diverse uses of coconut products in every day life. Every part of the coconut tree is of great utility and hence it is rightly called as '*kalpavriksha*' or the 'tree of heaven'. It is a source of several useful products.

The entry of coconut products in the export market, is a landmark in the history of India's export trade. In recent years, a large number of national programmes for coconut development have been launched in many Asian and Pacific countries, particularly in India, because coconut occupies an unique position in commercial agriculture as a fibre, food, oil seed and beverage crop.

This book has covered all the major segments of the subject and is divided into eight chapters spread over the following topics—Introduction and Design of the Study, Profile of the Study Area and Characteristics of the Sample Respondents, Review of Literature, Coconut Production—An Overview, Cost and Return Analysis, Marketing of Coconut, and Summary of Findings and Suggestions. I hope it would serve as a useful text and reference book for all categories of readers, particularly academics, researchers, practitioners and government agencies.

Any constructive criticism and suggestion is always welcome.

Dr. R. Mabel Sulochana
Dr. X. Antony Thanaraj

Contents

Introduction and Design of the Study

Introduction

Agriculture has been playing a predominant role in the economic development of all developed and developing countries. Ever since India's independence agriculture in India has taken strides owing to the varietal and agronomic interventions of agricultural research and the resourcefulness of the farming community. The Green Revolution of the 1960's ushered in rapid increases in food crop production such as wheat, rice and other cereals. Efforts were also taken to achieve similar increases in non-food crop production viz: coconut, groundnut, sugarcane, cotton etc. In recent years a large number of national programmes for coconut development have been launched in many Asian and Pacific countries, particularly in India because coconut occupies a unique position in commercial agriculture as a fibre, food, oilseed and beverage crop.[1] The high oil content of the endosperm of the coconut (copra) is widely used in both food and non-food industries like margarine and soaps. The coconut palm and its products are a major source of livelihood to a sizeable section of the rural folk in the tropics and also contribute substantially to the total export earnings of some of the Asian and Pacific countries. It is unique among horticulture crops of India because of the diverse uses of coconut products. Therefore, coconut production, productivity and marketing have become an attractive field for multidisciplinary research.

The Coconut Palm—The Kalpavriksha

The coconut palm, botanically known as 'Cocus nucifera' is unique among horticulture crops raised in India because of the diverse uses of the coconut products in everyday life. So far nearly 360 uses have been reported.[2] Extensively grown in tropical countries, the coconut tree or 'cocosnucifera' has multiple uses. Besides being an important oil seed crop, its raw nut and edible copra are important items of food. Coconut is an indispensable item offered in divine ablution. Tender coconut water is a refreshing unadulterated cool health drink. The coconut shell and husk are main raw materials for the manufacture of handicraft articles. Coconut leaves are used for thatching roofs and for making brooms. Husk is used for producing coir. Coconut milk, the aqueous extract of the solid coconut endosperm, plays an important role in the cuisines of South Asia and in the food industries. It is estimated that 25 per cent of the world's output of coconut is consumed as coconut milk.[3] The trunk of the tree is used as building material, fuel and for making utensils, furniture etc. In short, every part of the coconut tree is of great utility and hence it is rightly called as 'Kalpavriksha' or the 'Tree of Heaven'.[4]

Importance of Coconut Palm

Since Coconut is a multi-product crop, small and marginal farmers involved in coconut growing, depend solely on the palm for their domestic requirements such as food, fuel and shelter.[5] Among the coconut based industries, coir manufacture, copra making and oil milling are significant and coir products constitute one of the major items of export every year. Coconut occupies a place of importance in the social and religious functions of the people of India.[6] Coconut contributes over ₹ 7000 crores/year to the Gross Domestic Product of India and it earns foreign exchange to the value of

₹ 292 crores by way of export of coir and coir products. Coconut based farming system provides large quantity of biomass to satisfy the fuel requirements of a small family. As a result of diversification, coconut has become the main agro-based raw material for many industries producing new coconut products such as coconut cream, spray-dried coconut, coconut milk powder, tender coconut water, coconut vinegar etc. as well as for the manufacture of several handicrafts. In Kerala and Goa coconut toddy tapping is an important industry. Fermented toddy is used as an intoxicant in the west-coast of India. In Lakshadweep coconut toddy is used for producing vinegar and jaggery. In West Bengal 80 per cent of the nuts produced are consumed as tender nuts. In Karnataka coconut is used for making ball copra and desiccated coconut whereas in Tamil Nadu it is used for producing milling copra and coconut oil. Invariably in all the states of India, coconut is used in raw form or in dry form for various culinary preparations in households.[7]

Balakrishna Vaidyar *et al*, have highlighted the medicinal value of coconut. According to them coconut cabbage, the tender meristematic shoot in the heart of the crown is used in the treatment of *'Vatha'* and *'Pitha'*. Coconut inflorescence is used for curing urinary complaints, back pain and headache. Tender coconut water is effective in arresting dehydration and impotency. Coconut husk cures gynaecological diseases. Coconut kernel is good for increasing body weight and can be also used as an internal body cleaner. Coconut milk constitutes an ingredient of several ayurvedic preparations for treating skin and head diseases.[8]

Development of Coconut Trade

The history of coconut development and commercial exploitation of coconut products begins with the expansion of European soap and edible oil industry during the latter half of the 19th century. Increasing demand for coconut in the European market gave a Phillip to coconut cultivation in India and by the down of the 20th century India was in a formidable position in the export trade in copra and coconut oil. During the years 1909-1914 India exported about 31,000 tonnes of copra and 9000 tonnes of coconut oil annually. Since World War I exports of copra and coconut oil receded while imports gained momentum. Development of domestic soap industry combined with increased domestic consumption of coconut and coconut oil caused a deficit in the commodity.

Growing domestic demand for coconut necessitated governmental efforts to step up coconut production. With the establishment of the Coconut Research Stations at Nileshwar and Kasargod in 1916, coconut development activities attained a purposeful momentum. Genetic improvement of the crop and other efforts resulted in a slight increase of coconut area from 0.5 million hectares in 1920-21 to 0.57 million hectares in 1930-31.

Coconut production and trade assumed greater importance only after independence for the country. Under the Five Year Plans several development programmes were carried out for increasing production and productivity of coconut to cope up with the increasing demand for coconut and its by products. Besides meeting the domestic demand India's coconut production attained such an appreciable level of increase that coconut products made and entry into the export market. The major coconut based items of export are coir and coir products. Of late ice cream cups, spoons and forks are made of coconut shell, coconut oil in small packs, desiccated coconut, shell based charcoal and activated carbon, coir pith manure, coconut cake based cattle feed and coconut based handicrafts are also exported to the middle east and European countries on a limited scale. Table 1.1 shows the export of coconut products from India to various countries.

Table 1.1. Export of Coconut and Coconut Products from India to Various Countries

Sl.No.	Item	Exported to
1	Coconuts (fresh)	Bangladesh, Nepal, UAE, Kuwait, Mauritius, Qatar, Netherlands, Bahrain, Saudi Arabia, Germany and UK
2	Coconuts (dried)	Italy, Oman, Kuwait, Saudi Arabia, Spain, UAE, Iran, Mauritius, UK, USA, Nepal, Canada, Japan, Hongkong and Russia
3	Copra	Germany, Iran, Oman, Pakistan, UAE, Malaysia and USA
4	Desiccated Coconut	Afganistan, Argentina, Kuwait, UK, Brazil, Italy, Japan, Spain, Sudan, Oman, Saudi Arabia, Qatar, UAE and USA
5	Coconut Oil *a*. Crude Oil *b*. Refined Oil	Australia, Bahrain, Bangladesh, Jordan, UAE, Oman, Kenya, Kuwait, Nepal and Saudi Arabia Bangladesh, Bahrain, Brazil, Italy, Kuwait, Nepal, New Zealand, Oman, Saudi Arabia, USA and UK
6	Oil Cake (defatted)	Malaysia and Nepal
7	Coconut Shell (raw)	Canada, Italy, Japan, Kuwait, Saudi Arabia, Spain, Sri Lanka, Sweden, UK and USA
8	Shell Charcoal	Bhutan, Germany, Oman, Saudi Arabia, Italy, Singapore, Sri Lanka, Kenya, Netherland, Malaysia, Mauritius, Japan, USA, UAE and UK
9	Shell Hukah	Bahrain, Germany, Spain, Sri Lanka, Pakistan, Italy, USA and UAE

Source: Indian Coconut Journal, January 2003, p.32.

Export of Coconut Products from India

India's huge domestic market has been the main consumer of coconut and coconut products. The domestic price of coconut oil has so far been higher than the international price.

Table 1.2. Export of Coconut and Coconut Products from India *(Quantity in Tonnes, Value ₹ in Lakhs)*

Item	2003-2004		2004-2005		2005-2006		2006-2007		2007-2008	
	Qty	Value	Qty	Value	Qty	Value	Qty	Value	Qty	Value
Coconuts (Fresh)	610.32	70.08	935.34	100.73	1402.84	133.03	1043.41	161.16	2838.00	371.48
Coconuts (Dried)	594.61	299.07	583.80	256.28	608.71	233.25	622.39	241.15	982.20	250.72
Desiccated Coconut	332.07	68.56	431.93	49.28	652.16	113.05	312.06	72.17	1454.73	274.04
Other Coconuts excluding fresh/dried	196.96	55.12	796.42	168.46	678.02	227.71	758.63	240.59	3111.62	758.57
(*a*) Coconut oil (crude)	224.33	101.46	434.61	204.72	79.56	60.90	92.09	48.90	84.60	46.16
(*b*) Coconut oil (refined)	5789.24	2482.93	5519.75	2739.69	5298.27	2741.00	3584.74	2248.95	6732.29	3262.93
Other residues of Coconut or copra	196.00	16.26	3049.76	210.75	110.11	6.37	46.20	6.03	59.15	7.98
Oil Cake (defatted/ expellers)	285.62	32.94	1229.43	57.05	161.70	8.73	19.00	2.95	159.00	15.65
Coconut shell (raw)	266.36	83.16	301.61	75.50	601.84	192.64	673.20	205.44	499.07	102.34
Shell charcoal	9351.00	1109.12	2976.00	610.44	4869.00	641.38	10707.00	1327.41	17725	1226.50
Shell Hukah	73.71	12.73	4.40	1.37	8.06	7.09	22.27	43.59	60.42	45.16
Copra	—	—	—	—	—	—	1356.84	521.67	1671.46	539.53
Total	**17920.24**	**4261.43**	**16263.05**	**4474.27**	**14470.27**	**4365.15**	**19237.83**	**5120.01**	**35378.17**	**6901.06**

Source: Directorate General of Commercial Intelligence and Statistics, Kolkata.

Therefore, India has not had any significant role in the world trade. However, with the increase in the price of edible oils at the global level, the difference between the domestic and international price has been substantially reduced. On account of this, there has been an increase in the quantity of export of refined coconut oil compared to previous years. The export of desiccated coconut and shell charcoal also registered a sharp increase compared to the previous year. The export of coconut products from India for the last five years is given in Table 1.2.

India has no regular export trade in coconut oil. In India, the domestic demand for oils is more than the supply. The tendency, therefore, is to consume the entire production within the country itself. In the coconut oil export trade, Philippines occupies the monopoly position accounting for 60 per cent. From India, only a small quantity of coconut oil is exported to Bangladesh and Nepal, as part of trade agreements.

The export market of coconut in India has shown an increasing trend over the five years from 1997-1998 to 2001-2002. So there is wide scope for improving the export of coconut from India. The government has to take necessary steps for the improvement of coconut cultivation, maintenance, modernization and also to explore the possible opportunities for the betterment of Indian economy.

Statement of the Problem

Coconut is an important tropical oil seed crop, which gives coconut water, kernel, oilcake for cattle etc. Since, it is one of the leading commodities in agricultural exports, the production programme of the crop is of critical importance in improving the efficient use of resources. The cost of production and net return obtained per unit, would determine the profitability of the crop. The profitability of an enterprise depends upon the efficient use of the resources in production.

Though production is the initiation of the developmental process, it could bring less gain to the producers unless there exists an efficient marketing system. The producers depend upon the market conditions to fulfill their hopes and expectations. But forced sales, multiplicity of market charges, malpractices in unregulated markets and superfluous middlemen are the problems faced by the cultivators.

The market imperfection and the consequent loss in marketing efficiency are more pronounced in markets for perishable commodities which require quick transportation and better storage facilities. Though coconut has a pride, not only for its diverse uses but also for its special preference to consumers, both rich and poor, it is subjected to the above stated production and marketing problems. The Kanyakumari District of Tamilnadu is one of the rich coconut producing regions and hence the present study is an attempt to analyze the production and marketing of coconut in the district.

Scope of the Study

Coconut is a principal crop cultivated in Kanyakumari District. It contributes to the district's economic, social and cultural development in many ways. It is also a primary source of food to the people of the district.

Coconut provides the basic raw materials to the oil and coir industries in the district. The present study covers only production and marketing of coconuts and does not go into the industrial activities involving coconuts. The study has been undertaken from the point of view of the farmers, and market functionaries.

Objectives of the Study

The following are the specific objectives of the present study:

1. To study the profile of the study area and characteristics of the sample respondents;
2. To analyse the trend, growth and magnitude of variability of coconut production;
3. To analyse the cost and returns of coconut production;
4. To study the resource use efficiency and to compute returns to scale;

5. To evaluate the capital productivity of coconut cultivation;
6. To study the temporal variations in the price of coconut;
7. To evaluate marketing cost, marketing margin, price-spread and marketing efficiency of different channels;
8. To analyse the problems encountered in the cultivation and marketing of coconut by the growers and to suggest suitable solutions to solve them.

Operational Definition

Marginal Farmer

A 'marginal farmer' is a person, who is engaged either as an employer's single worker or family worker in the cultivation of land upto two and a half acres, either owned or held from government or private persons or institutions, for payment in cash, kind or share.

Small Farmer

A 'small farmer' is a person who is engaged in cultivation of 2½ to 5 acres either owned or held from government or private persons or institutions for payment in cash, kind or share.[9]

Large Farmers

A 'large farmer' is a person, who is engaged in cultivation of land above 5 acres of land, owned or held from government or private persons or institutions for payment in cash, kind or share.

Cultivator

A 'cultivator' is a person who is engaged either as an employer's single worker or family worker in cultivation of land owned or held from government or private persons or institutions for payment in money, kind or share. 'Cultivation' also includes supervision and direction of the work of cultivation. Similarly, persons engaged in the production of cereals and millets, such as paddy, wheat, jowar, bajra, ragi and other crops like sugarcane, ground nut, tapioca, pulses and raw jute, kindred fibre, cotton and other fibre crops are also considered as cultivators.

Agricultural Labourer

A person who works in another person's land for wages in money, kind or share should be regarded as an agricultural labourer. He or she has no risk in the cultivation, but merely works in another person's land for wages and has no right of lease or contract on land on which he or she works.

Literate

A person who can both read and write and understand any language, is a literate. A person who can merely read but cannot write is not a literate.

Cropping Pattern

'Cropping pattern' is the nature of crop in a single agricultural season.

Main Occupation

Main occupation of a household is that from which the head of the household derives the major annual income.

Allied Occupation

An occupation, other than the main occupation, is considered as secondary occupation or allied occupation.

Husk

'Husk' is the thick fibrous coating around the woody shell of a palm fruit. This husk is made use of in the manufacturing of various products of commercial importance.

Hybrid Varieties

The term refers to those varieties of coconut developed by inter-varietal crossing.

Edible Oil

Edible oil is the oil used in cuisines and catering establishments.

Edible Copra

Copra is used for various household sweet preparations and also as an ingredient in the processed betel nuts for chewing.

Milling Copra

Copra used for extracting oil is referred to as 'milling copra'.

Coconut

Coconut consists of an outer skin, which is green or brown in colour when harvested, enclosing a thick fibrous coating or husk. Inside the husk, there is a woody shell covering the kernel which is separated from it by a brown skin. The kernel is a solid white layer, preserving an aqueous liquid, known as coconut water.

Copra

It refers to the coconut kernel, processed from raw coconut after removing the lint and the shell. It is used for extracting oil. The oil content present in the copra is known as unctuous. It is used for various household preparations and also as an ingredient in the processing of betel nuts for chewing. The copra used for extracting coconut oil is called 'milling copra'.

Coconut Shell

It is the outer cover of coconut, made up of hardened cellulose. The activated carbon, manufactured from the coconut shell, is considered superior to the carbon contained in other materials such as coal, lignite, wood, paddy husk and the like. Shell charcoal, shell-based activated carbon, shell powder, shell handicrafts, shell ice-cream cups, ladles, forks, show pieces and shell buttons are the shell-based products.

Harvesting

Plucking and gathering the matured coconuts from the coconut tree is known as harvest. The harvesting operation is carried out by labourers, using traditional instruments.

Desiccated Coconut

It is a dehydrated coconut meat, in grated or shredded form, which is a convenient substitute for grated raw coconut.

Grading

It refers to the classification of coconuts, according to their size and quality. Grading is inevitable since the nuts are sold on the basis of their size and colour.

Coconut Farming

It means the cultivation of coconut, which is non-recurring in nature. Once the trees are planted they are nurtured carefully to get the yield.

Yield

The output received from the coconut tree is called yield. It denotes the number of nuts harvested from the tree.

Cost

Cost is a measurement, in monetary terms, of the amount of resources used for some purpose and the amount of expenditure incurred in the realization of the objective. The amount spent on developing the coconut palm and the upkeep of the same is known as cost.

Construction of Tools

The interview schedule used in this study has been structured below by the researcher.

With a view to identifying the variables for the study, the researcher had an in-depth review of the previous studies relating to the topic of the present study. The researcher also had a trial interview with five officers working in the office of the Department of Agriculture, Nagercoil, five educated coconut farmers and five uneducated farmers.

Based on the information collected from these sources, the first draft of the interview schedule was prepared. The draft schedule was handed over to a few faculty members, researchers and the educated farmers for their critical comments. In the light of their comments, the interview schedule was revised and the second draft was prepared. The second draft of the interview schedule was administered to the farmers who were included in the trial interview and a selected number of farmers from the four taluks of Kanyakumari District. Their suggestions regarding the format and word arrangements were incorporated in the interview schedule and the final draft was prepared.

Sampling Design

In Tamil Nadu, Kanyakumari District ranks first in area of cultivation and production of coconut. Hence this district was chosen for the selection of respondents.

Kanyakumari District, consists of four taluks and nine blocks, and one block from each taluk namely Thovalai, Rajakkamangalam, Kurunthancode and Munchirai were selected, based on area under coconut cultivation. From each block two panchayats were selected by simple random sampling. Accordingly, Neyyoor and Reethapuram were selected from Kurunthancode Block, Kollencode and Puthukadai from Munchirai Block, Azahia-pandipuram and Chempagaramanputhoor from Thovalai Block and Ganapathypuram and Thengamputhoor from Rajakkamangalam. From each panchayat selected, two villages were selected at random. These were the villages of Kadiapatinam and Lekshmi puram in Neyyoor Panchayat, Colachel and Thalakulam in Reethapuram, Eludesam and Kollencode in Kollencode, Painkulam and Arudesam in Puthukadai, Therisanam koppu, Arumanalloor in Azahiapandipuram, Chenpagaraman Puthoor and Ananthapuram in Chenpagaramanputhoor, Neendakarai and Vempannor in Ganapathipuram and Thengamputhoor and Tharmapuram villages in Thengamputhoor Panchayat. A sample of 192 coconut growers were selected at the rate of 12 from each selected village. It was found that 12 interview schedules were incomplete and hence rejected. Thus the total sample size was 180 consisting of 80 marginal farmers, 60 small farmers, and 40 large farmers. Thus Multistage Sampling Method was adopted in the selection of the District, Taluks, Blocks and Panchayats, followed by Simple Random Selection of villages and respondents.

For collecting data from the market functionaries, Convenience Sampling Technique was applied. The market functionaries included 10 village traders, 10 wholesalers and 10 retailers in each of the Development Blocks of Thovalai, Rajakkamangalam, Kurunthancode and Munchirai. The respondents in the terminal market at Vadasery comprised of 5 wholesalers and 5 retailers. Thus the total sample size is 130.

Collection of Data

The present study is based on both primary and secondary data. The primary data were collected from growers, through personal interview method. Based on physical, cultural and socio economic environment of farming in the region, interview schedule was designed, pre-tested and finalised.

Detailed informations were collected from the coconut growers on cropping pattern, labour utilization, age of the coconut trees, variety and number of coconut trees.

The data required for the study of marketing were also gathered by interviewing the different market functionaries using another well-structured pre-tested schedule. Informations were collected from the intermediaries on marketing cost, marketing margin, price-spread and problems in marketing. Data regarding price of coconut, area, production and other secondary data were collected from various journals, books, coconut statistics, published by

Coconut Board, Cochin, Statistical Year Book and the Reports of Director of Economics and Statistics, Ministry of Agriculture, New Delhi and Director of Economics and Statistics, Trivandrum.

Period of Study

Primary data were collected from coconut growers and merchant middle men. The study was undertaken during the months June to August 2008. Primary data collected from growers relate to the year 2008-09. Secondary data relating to prices, area under cultivation of coconut, production of coconut and productivity of coconut were collected for a period of 20 years from 1986-87 to 2005-06.

Tools of Analysis

Cobb-Douglas type of Production Function was used to analyse the determinants of coconut yield.

To evaluate the resource use efficiency in coconut cultivation, marginal value productivity of each of the input variables was equated with the acquisition cost.

To study the trends in the areas of cultivation, production and productivity of coconut, Simple Regression Equation has been used.

In order to find out the growth rate in area, production and productivity of coconut, compound growth rate has been calculated using Semi-log or Exponential Function.

To study the magnitude of variability in the area, production and productivity of coconut, Co-efficient of Variation has been computed.

Garrett's Ranking Technique has been used to analyse the problems in coconut cultivation and marketing of coconut.

To assess capital productivity involved in the investment in coconut cultivation, pay-back period, net present value and internal rate of return have been calculated.

To measure the marketing efficiency of the various channels in the marketing of coconut, Shepherds formula has been used.

Time Series Analysis has been carried out to study the temporal variations in the price of coconut, using Multiplicative Model.

Limitations of the Study

The study is confined to Kanyakumari District only. The researcher has depended on the information and data supplied by the coconut farmers who are not used to keeping proper records about cost of manures, seeds and the actual prices received for their produce. Hence. the study suffers from respondents' recall bias. These had been minimized by suitable interaction with the cultivators as well as cross checks then and there with the agricultural departmental field staff during the survey. Moreover, as the study is based on the opinions of the sample respondents, the results of the study cannot be generalized and should be used with caution.

Chapter Scheme

The present study is presented in seven chapters.

The first chapter entitled 'Introduction and Design of the Study' introduces the topic and traces the development of coconut trade. It also includes statement of the problem, objectives, concepts, sampling design, collection of data, tools of analysis, limitations of the study and chapter scheme.

The second chapter entitled 'Profile of the Study Area and Characteristics of the Sample Respondents' describes the geographical coverage of the sample district and the demographic features of the respondents.

The third chapter entitled 'Review of Literature' presents the findings of the previous studies related to coconut.

The fourth chapter entitled "Coconut Production—An Overview" deals with the growth rate, magnitude of variability and trend values in production, area and productivity of coconut in the major coconut producing countries in the world, India, Tamil Nadu and the study area.

The fifth chapter entitled 'Cost and Returns Analysis' analyses the cost of production, profitability, production function and capital productivity of coconut.

In the sixth chapter, 'Marketing of Coconut', the channels of distribution, price-spread, price analysis and the problems faced by the growers in marketing coconut are discussed.

The seventh chapter entitled, 'Summary of Findings and Suggestions' emphasizes the relevance of the study, presents the findings and puts forth some useful suggestions.

REFERENCES

1. Sugata Ghose, 'Coconut—India's Pride', *Kisan World*, Vol. 25, No.8, August, 1998, p. 31.
2. Working papers presented at the Third Session of FAO, 1969, p. 15.
3. Krishnakumar T. 'Some Facts About Coconut Milk', *Kisan World*, Vol.22, No.5, May 2005, p. 52.
4. Rajkumar S. and Thamilselvan R. 'Importance of Coconut Cultivation', *Kisan World*, Vol.32, No.5, May 2005, p. 58.
5. Thamban P.K. 'Coconut Industry in India', Asian and Pacific Coconut, CDB, Ministry of Agriculture, 1990, p. 1.
6. *Ibid* p. 7-8.
7. Singh H.P. 'Coconut Industry in India-Challenges and Opportunities', *Indian Coconut Journal*, Annual Number, Vol.29, No.4, 1998, pp. 4-11.
8. Balakrishna Vaidyar, *et al.*, 'Medicinal Uses of Coconut', *Indian Coconut Journal*, Vol. No. 33, No. 24, p. 2002.
9. *Tamil Nadu Agricultural Census Book*, 2005-06, p. 41-42.

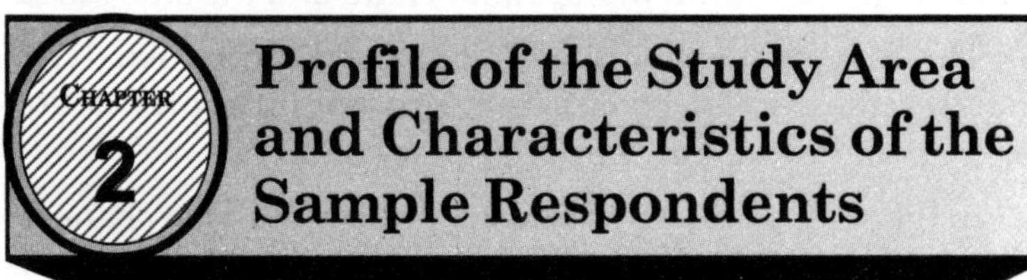

Profile of the Study Area and Characteristics of the Sample Respondents

This chapter offers a description of the study area—the Kanyakumari District, which was formerly the Southern Division of the erstwhile princely state of Travancore.

Formation of Kanyakumari District

The Southern Division of the State of Travancore consisted of four Tamil speaking taluks viz., Thovalai, Agasteeswaram, Kalkulam and Vilavancode. Since India's independence, the Tamil speaking people of this region started a people's movement, demanding the merger of the four taluks with the Madras State. Their long and protracted struggle culminated in the Constitution of the State Reorganization Commission in 1956. Based on the recommendations of the Commission, the Indian Parliament passed the State Reorganization Act in March 1959. This Act provided for the creation of a new district of the Madras State [Tamilnadu] called Kanyakumari District, consisting of the four Tamil speaking taluks. Accordingly, the Kanyakumari District was inaugurated on 1st November, 1959, with Nagercoil as headquarters.[1]

Location

Situated near the equator between 77.05′ and 77.36′ east longitude and between 8.03′ and 8.35′ north latitude, the Kanyakumari District is bounded on the north-east by the Thirunelveli District, Trivandrum District of the Kerala State on the north-west, the Arabian Sea on the west and the Indian Ocean and the Gulf of Mannar on the south and south-east respectively.[2]

Physical Features

Tucked away neatly at the southern end of the Indian Peninsula between the Western Ghats and the Arabian Sea, the Kanyakumari District, with its rich flora and fauna, has been a tourist attraction. With the influence of its situation near the equator, of its vicinity to the Indian Ocean, of its extensive sea-coast, of its mountain barrier that determines its climate conditions, its variety of natural scenery and verdant surroundings, of racial peculiarities, this coastal strip developed a distinctive culture and civilization of its own. The Western Ghats, the backbone of Southern India, gave the region a geographical insulation and inaccessibility to the outside world and contributed to its comparative immunity from molestation and conquest by the war-like races that swept over the rest of the Indian continent.[3]

The Western Ghats on the eastern side of the district run almost parallel to the western coast with an altitude ranging from 300′ to 6000′ above mean sea level and an unequal breadth diminishing from the north and converging to a point at its southern extremity. Mahendragiri and Muthukuzhivayal are the highest peaks with a height of 5700′ and 4400′ respectively.[4]

Area and Population

The total area of the Kanyakumari District is 1672 square miles and its population is 1669763, density being 999.[5] Free from serious threats from the great empire builders of the north and the east, the people of this region evolved an altogether amorphous social structure. The earliest inhabitants of the region were Dravidians.[6] Aryans are believed to have immigrated into the region around 10th century A.D.[7] The advent of the Aryans as well as the European colonists and merchants resulted in fusion of races and cultures which provide to the ethnologist a wider sphere for study in the varied and mutually contrasting manners and customs of the 420 castes of the population besides the mixed descendants of the Portuguese, the Dutch and other European nations.[8]

The split up figures for different categories of people of the district are given in Table 2.1 below:

Table 2.1. Different Categories of People in the Kanyakumari District

Total population	1669763
Male population	829542
Female population	840221
Rural population	1330240
Urban population	270109
Scheduled Caste	76862
Scheduled Tribe	5223
Literates	1148778
Male workers	395041
Female workers	69046
Rural workers	387350
Urban workers	76737
Cultivators	243710
Agricultural Labourers	177410
Household industries	13377
Other workers	235777
Marginal workers	224044
Non-workers	2218

Source: AGROSTAT, Joint Director of Agriculture, Kanyakumari, 2003, p.2

Climate and Rainfall

The Kanyakumari District is blessed with a favourable agro-climatic condition for the growth of different varieties of crop. In the plains semi-arid tropical monsoon type of climate prevails. The maximum and minimum temperatures are 37.5°C and 27.7°C respectively. Temperature shoots up further in April-May unless moderated by rains. The proximity of the Western Ghats and the sea as well as the south-west and north-east monsoons greatly influence the climate of the district.[9]

The monsoon rains and the winter and summer rains account for the average annual rainfall of 1352.5mm.[10] The annual average rainy days are normally 85.9 days. Hence the sorts of crop like food crops, plantain crops, cash crops, fibre crops and tuber crops are raised. The occurrence of the South West Monsoon from June to September and the North East Monsoon from October to December facilitate flourishing cultivation of crops. But for unusual and occasional failure of the monsoons, the Kanyakumari District has no water scarcity.[11] A season-wise distribution of rainfall and the annual average rainfall in the district are presented in Table.2.2.

Table 2.2. Season-wise Average Rainfall in Kanyakumari District

Season	Rainfall (mm)	Percentage to the Total
South-West Monsoon (June–September)	232.1	17.16
North-East Monsoon (October-December)	750.6	55.50
Winter (January-February)	28.2	2.09
Summer(March-May)	341.6	25.5
Total	**1352.50**	**100.00**

Source: AGROSTAT, 2003, p.11

The major source of rainfall is the North-East monsoon. As the monsoon rains supply adequate water for the cultivation of paddy, farmers of the district normally raise two crops annually. Though the summer and winter rains are not monsoon rains, they help to keep the climate temperate and enable the farmers to raise both food and non-food crops throughout the district. The average annual rainfall pattern is shown in Table 2.3 below:

Table 2.3. Average Annual Rainfall Pattern in Kanyakumari District

Year	Rainfall (mm)
1998	1980.30
1999	1703.70
2000	1598.00
2001	1628.08
2002	1352.50
2003	915.09
2004	1435.50
2005	1694.80
2006	1249.90
2007	1384.78

Source: District Statistical Office, Nagercoil.

The highest average annual rainfall in the district has been recorded as 1980.30 mm in 1998.

Natural Divisions

The Kanyakumari district is divided into three natural divisions. They are:

1. The mountain region along the Western Ghats in the Vilavancode and Kalkulam Taluks and the hill bases

called the high lands. This region is suited for raising crops like rubber, cloves, coffee, coconut, pepper and pineapple.

2. The 68 kilometer long sea coast in the extreme south and southwest called the low lands, which are ideal for growing coconut, cashew etc.
3. The undulating valley between the uplands and the lowlands known as midlands where coconut, tapioca, banana and paddy crops are abundantly cultivated. [12]

Soil

Besides the favourable climatic conditions of the Kanyakumari District, the soil conditions constitute the physical basis for agriculture. Contrasts in agriculture are caused by the differences in soil textures, drainage and fertility.[13] As far as Kanyakumari District is concerned soil conditions in the different parts of the district differ considerably within short distances. Sandy soil is found along the high lands; laterite soil in areas with high rainfall and red soil in the mid lands. Laterite soil with moisture holding capacity with varying amounts of aluminium hydroxide is found in the Thiruvattar, Munchirai, Kurunthankode, Rajakamangalam, Killiyoor, Thuckalay and Melpuram Blocks. The chief crops in these Blocks are tapioca, rubber, coconut and spices. Red soil has low moisture holding capacity and hence it is not as fertile as laterite soil. Mixed type of red and alluvial soil occurs in Agasteeswaram and Thovalai Blocks. [14]

Irrigation

Irrigation is essential for raising crops and for meeting the need for food and fibre. In Kanyakumari District, there are a few non-perennial rivers like the Paralayar, Kothayar, Thampiraparani, Valliyar, Chittar and Pazhayar.[15] Taking their origin from the Western Ghats and running across the gentle slopes of the mid lands, these rivers confluence with the waters of the Arabian Sea on the west.[16]

The rulers of Travancore bestowed great attention to irrigation from the beginning of the 20th century. They took steps to form storage reservoirs for impounding water for irrigation during periods of drought or insufficient rainfall.[17] The first of this kind was the Petchiparai Dam built across the Kothaiyar River in 1906. The Perunchani dam was constructed in the Paralaiyar River in 1953. These dams and a network of channels called the Kothaiyar System irrigate 25,900 hectares of double cropland in the district.[18] In order to increase the storage capacity of the Petchipparai and Perunchani dams two minor reservoirs namely Chittar I and Chittar II have been built. The Puthan Dam and the Pandian Dam across Paralayar as well as the Thirparapu and Aruvikkarai Dams are diversion weirs.

Table 2.4. Area Directly and Indirectly Fed by Channels

Sl. No.	Name of Channel	Total Designated Ayacut in Ha	Direct	Indirect	No. of Tanks
1.	Anandanar Channel	43432	2766	1466	147
2.	P.P.Channel	7977	5363	2614	472
3.	C.P. channel	4368	3097	1271	317
4.	N.P.Channel	3640	900	2740	71
5.	Thovalai channel	5208	3586	1622	102
6.	Pazhayar	2765	1869	896	24
7.	Thirparappu L.B.C	500	391	109	118
8.	Thirparappu R.B.C	475	329	146	18
9.	Aruvikkarai RBC	79	74	5	1
10.	Aruvikkarai LBC	315	242	73	42
11.	Neyyoor Channel	1457			
12.	Others	742			
	Total	**31758**	**18617**	**10942**	**1205**

Source: AGROSTAT, Joint Director of Agriculture, Kanyakumari, 2003, p. 126

Besides the reservoirs and a network of irrigation canals, there are in all 1205 tanks.[19] The percentage of area irrigated by tanks to the net area irrigated is 56.6 per cent.[20] The following Table 2.4 provides more particulars about the area directly and indirectly fed by channels, the total area covered being 10942 ha.

Revenue Divisions and Development Blocks

The two major Revenue Divisions of the district are Nagercoil and Padmanabhapuram[21] comprising Thovalai and Agastheeswaram taluks and Kalkulam and Vilavancode Taluks respectively. There are in all 81 revenue villages.[22]

In order to promote agricultural development the Kanyakumari District has been divided into 9 Development Blocks having their own headquarters as shown in Table 2.5.

Table 2.5. Development Blocks and their Headquarters

Sl. No.	Name of Taluk	Name of Block	Name of Head Quarters
1.	Thovalai	Thovalai	Thovalai
2.	Agastheeswaram	1. Rajakkamangalam 2.Agastheeswaram	Pazhavilai Perumalpuram
3.	Kalkulam	Thiruvattar Thuckalay Kurunthankode	Thiruvattar Kozhiporevilai Kurunthankode
4.	Vilavancode	Melpuram Munchirai Killiyoor	Pacode Munchirai Tholyavattam

Source: Credit Plan for Kanyakumari District, Lead cell, IOB, 1990-91

Cropping Pattern

The Kanyakumari District is very suitable for the cultivation of a variety of crops. Important food crops are paddy, tapioca and oil seeds like groundnut and coconut. Cashew, rubber fruits and spices are the commercial crops raised in the district. Of the entire crops paddy occupies a predominant position, covering an area of 31000 hectares (both crops). Coconut follows paddy covering an area of about 22586 hectares. Rubber is the chief commercial crop, occupying 18327 hectares. Details of area and productivity of each of the main crops are provided in Table 2.6.

Table 2.6. Normal Area and Productivity of Major Crops

Sl. No.	Name of the Crop	Area (in ha)	Normal Yield (kg/ha)
1.	Paddy	31000	6900
2.	Coconut	22586	10000 nuts
3.	Rubber	18327	1200
4.	Tapioca	9000	15000
5.	Banana	5100	25000
6.	Pulses	3500	250
7.	Cashew	1800	2000
8.	Mango	1750	20000
9.	Tamarind	1731	5.6 MT
10.	Jack	754	30.40 MT
11.	Arecanut	750	500000 nuts
12.	Clove	518	1250 to 2500 kgs
13.	Pepper	113	1500 kgs
14.	Pineapple	18	30.40 MT

Infrastructural Facilities

Infrastructural facilities include trade, marketing, storage, transportation and communication, credit institutions, research centres and extension agencies. The most important trade centre in the Kanyakumari district is Kottar. In early days pepper, ivory, teak, sandalwood, rosewood and fruits were the commodities of commerce,[23] but at present, Kottar is an important paddy-milling centre.[24]

Though industrial development in the Kanyakumari District is still a dream, small scale industries are coming up. In this, coconut industry has a greater role to play. Coconut oil crushing with the help of bullock drawn country chekku in the village settlements of Vaniars and Chekkalars at Asaripallam, Colachel, Eathenkadu, Eraniel, Kannamangalam, Manvalakurichi, Perumkode and Pudukkadai has been an important cottage industry. Coconut husks are the main raw material for coir and coir based industries. Coir production centres are found along the coastal strip from Manakkudi to Kollencode. Coir and coir based products are supplied to the local markets and to other commercial centres of Kerala, Karnataka, Andhra Pradesh, Orissa and Tamilnadu. Mat and mattings are also exported to foreign countries.

The Kanyakumari District has a well-developed network of roads. The Chennai-Nagercoil-Trivandrum national highway passes through this district covering a distance of 62.4 km.[25] Besides the national highway and the state highways, district roads and rural roads, provide adequate facilities for the passenger and goods transport. The first rail route from Kuzhithurai West to Nagercoil and the branch line from Nagercoil to Kanyakumari were opened on 16th April, 1979. Rail link from Kanyakumari to the Himalayan border was inaugurated on 3rd August 1984.[26]

From the early centuries of the Christian era, Kanyakumari served as a harbour.[27] Manakudy and Rajakkamangalam were also important ports and trade centres. Muttom was a leading centre of foreign trade.[28] Colachel on the west coast still continues to be a natural port engaged in export trade, the chief exports being palmirah fibre, mineral sands fish and salt.[29]

Postal and telecommunication system in the district provides communication facilities to almost all the villages and towns.

Credit and finance facilities are extended to the people of the district by about 123 commercial and cooperative banks. They provide investment credit for minor irrigation, land development, farm mechanization, plantation, horticulture and wasteland development and production credit in the form of loans. The central cooperative bank, Nagercoil with its 16 branches extend easy credit to the farmers.[30]

There are in all 19 Agricultural Extension Centres including 10 sub-centers. They are functioning under the supervision and control of four Assistant Directors of Agriculture. Particulars regarding these centers are given in Table 2.7 below:

Table 2.7. Agricultural Extension Centres in Kanyakumari District

	Agricultural Extension Centres	
	Main Centres	**Sub Centres**
Nagercoil	Nagercoil Perumalpuram	Suchindram Theroor Eraviputhoor Anjugramam
Bhoothapandy	Thovalai	Sahayanager
Thuckalay	Kurunthancode Kozhiporvilai Thiruvattar	Monday Market Thuckalay Kumarapuram
Vilavancode	Killiyoor Munchirai Melpuram	Karungal Thoduvetti

Source: Agrostat, 2003, p.8

Characteristics of the Sample Respondents

This section is devoted to a discussion of the socio-economic characteristics of the 180 sample coconut cultivators such as age, education, occupation, family size, operational holdings, number of family members engaged in farming and experience in farming, so as to have a fair knowledge about them, to make meaningful inferences.

Taluk-wise Classification

In Kanyakumari District, coconut is cultivated in all the four taluks and the coconut palms are owned by small, medium and large farmers. Table 2.8 exhibits the sample respondents of the four taluks selected for the present study.

Table 2.8. Taluk-wise Classification of Respondents

Taluk	Marginal farmers	Small farmers	Large farmers	Total
Agastheeswaram	21 (26.25)	16 (26.7)	20 (50)	57 (31.6)
Thovalai	17 (21.25)	16 (26.7)	8 (20)	41 (22.8)
Kalkulam	26.0 (32.5)	17 (28.3)	7 (17.5)	50 (27.8)
Vilavancode	16 (20)	11 (18.3)	5 (12.5)	32 (17.8)
Total	**80 (100)**	**60 (100)**	**40 (100)**	**180 (100)**

Source: Survey Data
Figures in brackets are percentage of the total

It is observed from Table 2.8 that, 31.6 per cent of the sample respondents have been selected from Agastheeswaram Taluk and 27.8 per cent from Kalkulam Taluk. Among the marginal sample farmers, 32.5 per cent were selected from Kalkulam Taluk and 26.25 per cent from Agasteeswaram Taluk.

In the case of small farmers, 28.3 per cent belongs to Kalkulam Taluk whereas 26.7 per cent each from both Agastheeswaram and Thovalai Taluks. Out of 40 large farmers, 20 respondents (50 per cent) belong to Agastheeswaram Taluk. Thus it is clear from the table, that majority of the total sample respondents selected for the study, are marginal farmers.

Age-wise Classification

Age of the respondent is an important factor, which influences the pattern of cultivation and marketing. The age-wise distribution of the sample farmers is given in Table 2.9.

Table 2.9. Age-wise Classification of Sample Respondents

Age (in years)	Marginal farmers	Small farmers	Large farmers	Total
Below 30	2 (2.5)	3 (5)	2 (5)	7 (3.88)
30-40	25 (31.25)	24 (40)	11 (27.50)	60 (33.33)
41-50	21 (26.25)	19 (31.66)	11 (27.50)	51 (28.33)
Above 50	32 (40)	14 (23.33)	16 (40)	62 (34.45)
Total	**80 (100)**	**60 (100)**	**40 (100)**	**180 (100)**

Source: Survey Data
Figures in brackets are percentage of the total

Table 2.9 shows that 34.45 per cent of the sample respondents are in the age group of above 50 years whereas 33.33 per cent are in the age group of 30-40 years. Among the 80 marginal farmers, 32 (40 per cent) belong to the age group of above 50 years while it is 25 (31.25 per cent) fall in the age group of 30-40. Out of 60 small farmers, 24 (40 per cent) farmers are in the 30-40 years age group, whereas 31.6 per cent belong to 41-50 years age group. In the case of large farmers, 40 per cent of the respondents fall under the age group of above 50 years and 27.50 each in both 30-40 years and 41-50 years age groups.

Thus it is clear from the table that majority of the marginal and large farmers are in the age group of above 50 years.

Farming Experience

The experience of farmers in the cultivation of coconut is one of the deciding factors for the success of coconut cultivation and marketing. Table 2.10 shows the classification of sample farmers based on their farming experience.

Table 2.10. Experience of Sample Farmers in Coconut Cultivation

Experience (in years)	Marginal farmers	Small farmers	Large farmers	Total
Upto 10 years	25 (31.25)	17 (28.3)	7 (17.5)	49 (27.2)
11-20 years	38 (47.5)	36 (60)	16 (40)	90 (50)
21-30 years	11 (13.75)	4 (6.7)	10 (25)	25 (13.9)
31-40 years	6 (7.5)	3 (5)	7 (17.5)	16 (8.9)
Total	**80 (100)**	**60 (100)**	**40 (100)**	**180 (100)**

Source: Survey Data
Figures in brackets are percentage of the total

It is observed from Table 2.10 that, 50 per cent, 27.2 per cent and 13.9 per cent of the sample farmers have had the experience of 11-20 years, upto 10 years and 21-30 years respectively. It is apparent from the table that majority of the marginal, small and large farmers have 11-20 years experience in coconut cultivation.

Literacy Level

Literacy levels of the coconut cultivating farmers influence the method of cultivation, marketing, farm management and the like. Table 2.11 exhibits the sample respondents based upon their literacy level.

Table 2.11. Literacy Level of Sample Respondents

Literacy level	Marginal farmers	Small farmers	Large farmers	Total
Illiterate	7 (8.75)	6 (10)	5 (12.5)	18 (10)
School level	27 (33.75)	18 (30)	14 (35)	59 (32.8)
College level	34 (42.5)	24 (40)	14 (35)	72 (40)
Professional & Others	12 (15)	12 (20)	7 (17.5)	31 (17.2)
Total	**80 (100)**	**60 (100)**	**40 (100)**	**180 (100)**

Source: Survey Data
Figures in brackets are percentage of the total

Table 2.11 reveals, that 40 per cent of the farmers in the study area had college level education and 32.8 per cent had school education and 32.8 per cent and 17.2 per cent had professional or school education respectively. Hence it is apparent from the table that, percentage of farmers with college level education is higher in all the three categories of marginal, small and large farmers.

Occupation

The economic position of one's life is known by one's occupation. Occupation means the work that a person does to earn a living. The occupation of the coconut farmers is also an important factor influencing their level of attitude to coconut farming.

Table 2.12. Occupation of Sample Respondents

Occupation	Classification of Farmers			
	Marginal farmers	Small farmers	Large farmers	Total
Agriculture	70 (87.5)	53 (88.3)	34 (85.0)	157 (87.2)
Allied	10 (12.5)	7 (11.7)	6 (15)	23 (12.8)
Total	**80 (100)**	**60 (100)**	**40 (100)**	**180 (100)**

Source: Survey data
Figures in brackets are percentage of the total

Table 2.12 indicates that, about 87.2 per cent of the sample respondent cultivators had agriculture as their prime occupation. Among the marginal farmers 87.5 per cent were agriculturalists while 85 per cent of large farmers were agriculturalists. Further the table shows that 12.8 per cent of the respondents had agriculture as their allied activities. Thus, it is found from the table that agriculture is the occupation of majority of the sample respondents, selected for the present study.

Family Size

The family size is a significant factor in determining the availability of family labour in coconut farming operations. The family size of marginal, small and large farmers are given in Table 2.13.

Table 2.13 shows that, 36.7 per cent of the sample respondents have 4 members and 26.1 per cent have 3 members in their family. Among the marginal farmers, 37.5 per cent have a family of 4 members and 30 per cent have a family of only three members. Out of 40 large farmers, 40 per cent of the farmers have only 4 members in their family.

Thus it is inferred from the below table that majority of the marginal, small and large farmers have only four members in their family.

Table 2.13. Family Size of Sample Respondents

No. of family members	Marginal farmers	Small farmers	Large farmers	Total
2	8 (10)	9 (15)	4 (10)	21 (11.7)
3	24 (30)	16 (26.7)	7 (17.5)	47 (26.1)
4	30 (37.5)	20 (33.3)	16 (40)	66 (36.7)
5	14 (17.5)	11 (18.3)	10 (25)	35 (19.4)
6	4 (5)	4 (6.7)	3 (7.5)	11 (6.1)
Total	**80** **(100)**	**60** **(100)**	**40** **(100)**	**180** **(100)**

Source: Survey Data
Figures in brackets are percentage of the total

Number of Family Members Engaged in Coconut Cultivation

Family labour is the most important factor that determines productivity. The reason is that they work hard sincerely, irrespective of the time spent on farming. Table 2.14 shows the number of family members of the respondents, engaged in coconut cultivation.

It is evident from Table 2.14 that, 53.9 per cent of the sample respondents have utilized the services of only one family member in farming, 40 per cent have utilized two members and only a meagre 2.2 per cent of the farmers utilized four members in agricultural operations on their farms. Thus, it is understood from the above table that majority of the sample respondents have utilized one or two family members in coconut cultivation.

Table 2.14. Number of Family Members Engaged in Coconut Cultivation

No. of family members	Marginal farmers	Small farmers	Large farmers	Total
1	51 (63.8)	27 (45)	19 (47.5)	97 (53.9)
2	27 (33.7)	28 (46.6)	17 (42.5)	72 (40)
3	1 (1.25)	4 (6.7)	2 (5)	7 (3.9)
4	1 (1.25)	1 (1.7)	2 (5)	4 (2.2)
Total	**80 (100)**	**60 (100)**	**40 (100)**	**180 (100)**

Source: Survey Data
Figures in brackets are percentage of the total

Conclusion

Richly endowed with a favourable climate and soil condition conducive to coconut cultivation, Kanyakumari District offers scope for an increasing production and productivity of coconut palm. In spite of this, the farmers are attracted to raising rubber crop and the consequent conversion of coconut palm groves into rubber plantation has given a stunning blow to coconut production. Still coconut continues to occupy the second place in importance with regard to area of cultivation, production and productivity of coconut.

REFERENCES

1. Sridhar Menno, *Trivandrum District Gazetteer*, 1962, p. 5.
2. Kunjan Pillai P.N. *Studies in Kerala History,* Kottayam, 1970, p. 9.
3. Samuel Mateer, *The Land of Charity,* John Snow & Co, London, 1871, p. 13.
4. Nagam Aiya V. *The Travancore State Manual*, Vol.1, Government Press, Trivandrum, 1906, p.11.
5. *AGROSTAT*, Joint Director of Agriculture, Kanyakumari, 2003, p.2.
6. *Imperial Gazetteer of India*, Vol.1, p. 447.
7. Kusuman K.K. *Slavery in Travancore*, KHS, Trivandrum, 1973, p. 25.
8. Samuel Mateer, *op.cit.,* pp.1-2.
9. Census of India, *Madras District Census Handbook*, Kanyakumari, 1981, p. 4.
10. *AGROSTAT*, 2003, p. 4.
11. Pillay K.K. *Suchindrum Temple*, Madras, 1953, p. 2.
12. Narayana et al, "An Approach to the Study of Irrigation—A Case Study of Kanyakumari District", *Economic and Political Weekly*, Vol. XVII, No.9, September, 1882, p. 82.
13. Shrila D.W. *Agricultural Geography of Great Britain*, Sangamon Press, Oxford, 1971, p. 20.
14. *Credit Plan for Kanyakumari District*, Lead cell, I.O.B, 1988-1990, p. 3.
15. *Gazetteers of India*, Kanayakumari District, 1995, p. 291.
16. *The Travancore Directory for 1938*, Government of Travancore, Trivandram, 1938, p. 108.
17. *Irrigation Project of Kerala*, Public Works Department, Government of Kerala, 1947, p. 1.
18. *Gazetteers of India*, Kanyakumari District, 1995, pp. 295-297.
19. *AGROSTAT*, Joint Director of Agriculture, Kanyakumari District, 2003, p. 126.
20. *Gazetteers of India*, Kanyakumari District, 1995, p. 271-272.
21. *Statistical Hand Book of Tamil Nadu*, 1985, p. 91.

22. *Village Register*, Joint Director of Agriculture, Kanyakumari.

23. *Gazetteers of India*, Kanyakumari District, p. 481.

24. Census of India, *Kanyakumari District Census Hand Book*, Parts XIII, A and B, 1981, p.14.

25. *Gazetteers of India*, Kanyakumari District, 1995, p. 505.

26. *Ibid.,* pp. 503-504.

27. Pillay K.K., *op.cit,* p. 15.

28. Padmanabhan S. *The Contribution of Kanyakumari to the Tamil World*, 1981, p. 3.

29. Gazetteers of India, Kanyakumari Dist, 1995, p. 482.

30. *4th Annual Report, Kanyakumari Central Co-operative Bank Ltd.,* 2002-2003, pp. 8-9.

Review of Literature

The review of the earlier studies and the experience of the researchers help one in evaluating the strength and weakness of the concepts used earlier. An attempt is made here to review several such studies and specify appropriate concepts as applicable to the present study.

Production and Production Technology of Coconut

S. Rajkumar and R. Thamil Selvan in their study entitled 'Importance of Coconut Cultivation' pointed out the significance of coconut as a source of edible oil and as an agro-based raw material for many industries such as manufacture of shell powder, and handicrafts. Fermented coconut toddy is an intoxicant used widely in the west coast of India. Vinegar and jaggery are important by – products of coconut toddy. The tree trunk is used as a building material and for making furniture. Fifty per cent of the total coconut production is converted into copra. Coconut crop is raised in India under varying soil and climatic conditions in 17 states and 3 Union Territories. As the coconut tree is versatile in its adaptability to wide range of soil conditions, coconut cultivation has begun to spread from the west coast of India to interior regions of Tamil Nadu especially to Erode District and Thanjavur District.[1]

In an indepth study of coconut development in India, Sugata Ghose traces the different stages of coconut development. Expansion of European soap and edible oil companies offered great opportunity to India to export copra in the latter half of the 19th century. Steady increase in export trade enhanced the pace of coconut development. On the eve of the First World War, India was one of the leading exporters of copra, the annual quantum of export being 30 tonnes of copra and 10,000 tonnes of coconut oil. But the post war period witnessed fall in prices. The Second World War worsened the situation. Hence the Government of India set up the Central Coconut Committee in 1945. It did yeomen service for the growth of coconut sector. In 1966 this committee was replaced by the Directorate of Coconut Development. But its powers and objectives were restrictive in processing and marketing aspects and so Parliamentary Act was passed in 1979 which provided for the formation of the Coconut Development Board, which was formed in January 1981. Since the formation of the Board, systematic crop research resulted in the introduction of hybrid coconut varieties. Further optimum manorial and cultural requirements of coconut were determined. Coconut processing technology received greater attention. Major technologies developed were (1) Imparting roasted flavour to coconut oil (2) Production of non-carbonated beverage from mature coconut water (3) Preservation and packing of tender coconut water (4) pollution free quicker wetting of fresh husk in cement tanks for extraction of white fibres (5) Production of vinegar and nata-de-coco from mature coconut water (6) Production of tannin, lignins, and other compounds from husks (7) coir net and geo-textiles for prevention of soil erosion and land-slides (8) light weight bricks and fuel briquets from coir pith (9) Extraction of lignosulphanates from coir pith (10) Coconut shell or cellular blocks are used in concrete masonry unit (11) Composting of coir pith to organic manure by edible mushroom (12) Production of coconut cream and coconut milk powder. (13) Production of activated carbon from coconut shell by fluidized bed technique. (14) Development of mechanical coconut dehuskers and coconut palm climbing device.

Traditionally, in India coconut was processed to coir, copra and coconut oil. In recent decades manufacturing of edible ball copra and desiccated coconut has gained some importance. Though a few units have been set up for manufacturing shell powder, shell characoal, activated carbon and different shell and wood handicrafts, processing of wet kernel into different edible products of commercial importance has not yet become popular. The researcher concludes the study with an optimistic note that in all the aspects of the coconut crop development, product marketing in domestic and export sector and processing technology, there is much scope for further development. Future strategy of the Central and State Governments should be focused to technology development, market expansion and productivity improvement.[2]

S.S. Nagarajan has found from a study of coconut productivity in the Rangasamudram Village of the Coimbatore District of Tamil nadu, that 75 West Coast Tall variety palms per acre receiving regularly both organic and inorganic manures at the rate of 30 kgs of farm yard manure, 1 kg of urea, 2 kgs each of super phosphate and muriate of potash, 1 kg of micro-nutrient mixture and 2kgs of powdered neem cake per palm per year has resulted in a yield of 100 nuts per tree per year. The nuts are sold locally at an average price of ₹ 4 per nut. The annual cultivation cost per acre is ₹ 12,000 Gross revenue is around ₹ 30,000 and the net income is ₹ 18,000. But after application of silt over the entire extent of the garden prior to the onset of the monsoon every year, productivity per tree increased to 120 nuts/yr., raising the total revenue per acre to ₹ 36,000 at an additional cost of ₹ 3,000. Net income per acre rose from ₹ 18,000 to ₹ 21,000. Nagarajan concludes that regular application of silt containing organic matter stimulates soil life, helps multiplication of earthworms and improvement of physical properties of soil. Ultimately use of synthetic fertilizers can be minimized or even dispensed with as this system depends on the primary production capacity of the soil and positive biotic interactions. It is also suggested that raising intercrops like banana and turmeric will fetch more income for the coconut farmer.[3]

Sugata Ghose gives a brief sketch of the different stages in the progress of coconut production in India since independence and points out the encouraging trend after the formation of the Coconut Development Board in 1981. The efforts of the Board resulted in increase in production and productivity and by 1996 total production was 13.9 billion nuts with the index reaching the all time high of 425.6 points. Productivity increased to 7779 nuts per hectare. Eventhough a slight decrease occurred during 1996 to 98 total production was maintained at the level of 13 billion nuts and India became the highest producer of coconut in the world. [4]

Jose Mathew advocates the advantages of Drip Fertigation as a successful technology for integrating irrigation and fertilization. According to him, irrigation and fertilization are the two most critical management factors that influence growth, yield and quality of agricultural crops. The use efficiency of these inputs is very low in India i.e 30 to 40 per cent. This leads to low crop productivity, degradation of soil health, and increased environmental pollution apart from the wastage of substantial quantity of these costly and scarce inputs. Adoption of Drip Fertigation technology has opened up new possibilities to optimize and integrate the use of water and fertilizer enabling to harness high crop yield and ensuring a healthy soil and environment.[5]

R. Veeraputhiran suggests the following strategies to implement drip irrigation which will improve irrigation efficiency to 80 to 90 per cent (1) Allocation of government subsidy for drip irrigation (2) simplified procedure for the disbursement of subsidy (3) reduction of gestation period to avail subsidy.

Veeraputhiran recommends fertigation for applying fertilizers under drip irrigation and herbigation as a new method of weed management. He concludes that drip irrigation system is highly suitable for adoption in growing trees and fruit trees, wide-spaced and commercial crops and that there is great prospect for rapid expansion of area under drip irrigation in the 21st century.[6]

Outlining the water saving irrigation methods followed to supplement the age old surface irrigation method such as Sprinkler/Overhead Irrigation Method and Micro or Drip Irrigation, R.K. Sivanappan concludes that in view of the scarcity of water, it is essential to manage water efficiently for all crops and he recommends the use of drip irrigation for all crops in all soils, particularly for wide spaced high value commercial crops like coconut, grapes, vegetables and fruit crops.[7]

V. Rajagopal et al., of the Central Plantation Crops Research Institute, Kasargod, Kerala dealt at length with the distinctive features of coconut, its strength and weaknesses as a perennial crop. According to him in coconut largest number of germ plasm is available for effective utilization to increase productivity and for breeding disease resistant varieties. Moreover, there is greater scope for the adoption of new technologies and community level approach for augmenting farm income. Coconut development is a potential source for women empowerment through self-help groups. According to these researchers the availability of time-tested and proven technologies for adoption at the farmers level provides scope for inter/multi/mixed crops in coconut farms. Coconut products and by products of high economic value are potentials for export and earnings in international markets. But decline in farm income imposed by factors such as fluctuating market price, pests and diseases, adverse climatic conditions, non-competitiveness at the global level and decline in general price level of coconut products at the international level are some of the threats faced by coconut industry. To overcome these threats, these researchers suggest certain macro and micro level strategies. At the macro level discouraging area expansion under coconut, increasing the productivity effect on production in the major coconut growing zones and checking the flow of imports by imposing rational import tariff rates will help to maintain a well stablilised price structure for coconut and its products. At the micro level emphasis should be on the theme 'competitiveness through higher productivity in production, processing and marketing sectors'. Replanting of senile and unproductive plants through high yielding varieties and hybrids, adoption of integrate nutrient management strategies, water management techniques and integrated pests and disease management strategies are some of the major technologies for realizing sustainable increase in productivity.

These researchers are of the view that coconut based cropping/farming systems assume great significance at present because coconut farmers are facing higher degree of production and price risks. Since coconut is a crop with wider spacing and ideal rooting pattern and canopy of coverage, coconut farming offers much scope for integrating a variety of crop combinations in the inter spaces. The study is concluded with the suggestion that in order to achieve economies of scale in coconut production it is advisable to venture into coconut farming on cooperative basis involving farm women. The research and development agencies should continue to strive for attaining excellence in their respective mandates for achieving sustainable development and improved standard of living of small and marginal coconut farmers in the country.[8]

Reviewing the progress of coconut production in India over the past five decades, P. Rethinam points out that, India is the third largest coconut producing country in terms of area and production. Coconut area in the country increased from 0.62 million hectares in 1950-51 to 1.82 million hectares in 2002 and production increased from 3281.7 million nuts to

12, 821.7 million nuts and productivity from 5238 to 6776nuts/ha/yr. While the area and production increased considerably, the increase in productivity was only marginal. The traditional cultivation practices, old and senile nature of nearly 45 per cent of the palms and the problems of root wilt disease as well as the Ercophyrid Mite are the major causes for the decline in productivity. Rethinam suggests the following strategies to enhance coconut productivity: (1) Scientific planting (2) Selection of proper variety suited for various situations (3) Adoption of the average management practice (4) Timely application of manures, fertilizers and water (5) Production of quality seedlings by farmers (6) Quality control of seedlings by government agencies before distribution for planting.[9]

According to Sugata Ghose the most common indicator used to understand the crop situation of a country are area and production. But the per capita availability is also an important criterion. The Production Population Ratio (PPR) of coconut in India steadily increased from 9.92 coconuts per head (CPH) in 1951 to 10.56cph in 1961 and to 11.08 cph in 1971 but dropped beyond the 1951 level by 1981 to 8.37 cph due to various constraints. The situation improved during the eighties and the PPR increased to an all time high of 11.49 cph by 1991. Among the 13 coconut producing states, the PPR of Lakshadweep was at the maximum of 512.60 cph followed by Andaman and Nicobar Isalnds with 289.57 cph and Kerala with 156.06 cph. Maharashtra had the lowest PPR of 1.38 cph.[10]

A. Christopher Lourduraj et al., point out the decline in coconut production in Kerala and the increasing trend in area and production in Tamil Nadu. According to them the increasing trend in Tamil Nadu is due to changing trends in agriculture, non-availability of labour, escalation of wages, conversion of area under annual crops into coconut plantations, higher profits from coconut etc. Based on the survey conducted in the Pollachi Tract in 1991, these researchers attribute decline in productivity to lack of interest on the part of the small and medium farm holders in irrigating or fertilizing the plantations and negligence in taking timely plant protection measures. These researchers suggest regular fertilization and plant protection are a must to increase productivity. According to them the possibility of utilizing coconut by-product and land use efficiency by planned intercropping have contributed to the increase in coconut area.[11]

R. Halli is optimistic about the scope for India to improve and increase her coconut production. Coconut research concept initiated in the Nileswar Coconut Farm in Kerala as far back as 1916 became a centre of global attraction during 1934-1936. In this farm the first hybrid coconut seedlings were produced under the guidance of J.S. Patel of the Department of Agriculture of the Madras State. But the coveted discovery only remained as an achievement of the researchers for some time. The credit of effecting a break through by giving shape to the largest Hybrid Coconut Seed Garden on the picturesque plains of Kodimanagalam near Nagamalai, 17 miles away from the temple city of Madurai, goes to the large hearted scientists of the Central Plantation Crop Research Institute and the Coconut Development Board of India. In this farm seed nuts are collected every month from about 4000 tall and 7500 parent palms once the nuts attain 12 months maturity. Seed nuts, thus collected give over 90 per cent true seedlings. The D and T hybrid seedlings produced by crossing Malyan Dwarf X Tiptur Tall, Malayan Dwarf X Andarman Ordinary, Malayan Dwarf X West Coast Tall, and Malayan Dwarf X East Coast Tall have excellent performance. They start flowering from the third year. The genetic potentiality of hybrids and their high yielding capacity have revolutionized coconut production. The commercial production of coconut seedlings will certainly lead India to greater heights in the global coconut production front and even open opportunities to export labelled hybrid seedlings to the other coconut producing countries.[12]

R.P.Iyer, E.V.V Bhaskara Rao and M.P.Govinda Kutty are of the opinion that the rural economy of the state is very much dependent upon coconut production, processing and marketing. Even though it is very difficult to ensure information on productivity of a crop like coconut, there is evidently a decline in yield. However, they are optimistic that the present efforts to preserve the high yield potential in subsequent generations of non-propotent elite palms through tissue culture will be rewarding if only growers extend their cooperation for carrying out scientific investigation for taking coconut to new levels of productivity.[13]

E.A.Parameswar Gupta holds the view that coconut occupies a unique place in the socio-economic life of the people of the Indian sub-continent. According to him India would emerge as the second largest producer of coconut in the world before the close of the twentieth century.[14]

Dealing at length with the varied uses of coconut palm products V.T. Markose, Chief Coconut Development Officer of the Coconut Development Board, Kochi says that coconut contributes more than ₹ 7000 crores annually to the GDP. The importance of coconut as a food item may be gauged from the fact that 60 per cent of its production is consumed in households as raw nut. Its by-products are utilized for making value added products. Although coconut has assumed considerable significance in our national economy, proper technology needs to be developed for utilizing coconut and other palm products like husk, timber, shell and leaves. Being an environmentally friendly tree, which can adapt to a wide range of soil types it offers employment opportunities to about 10 million people. With the development of value added products like coconut cream, coconut honey, coconut skimmed milk, tender coconut water, etc, coconut offers ample investment opportunities also. The researcher says that the mineral water boom in the country is an indication of the scope for increasing the use of tender coconut water as a natural soft drink. Since the coconut products are in great demand in the domestic and international market, there arises the urgent need to develop the technology of quality improvement and exploit the vast potential to earn valuable foreign exchange through exports. He is optimistic that with the advancement in technology, product diversification and byproduct utilization, the coconut industry in India has a luminant future. Markose suggests that with the change in the planting system and a reduction of planting density, different food crops and spices can be successfully introduced under a coconut based farming system so as to augment the production of food and spices crops along with coconut.[15]

E.A.Parameswara Gupta conducted an in-depth study on the trend in area, production and productivity of coconut in India with special reference to Karnataka. He says that the majority of coconut holdings in our country are very small and 98 per cent of them are less than 2 hectares. Small and marginal farmers form a sizeable portion of the coconut farming community. The area under coconut showed an impressive rise during 1955 to 1971, but the growth rate declined in the seventies and eighties. The area under coconut declined from 2689.49 thousand acres to 2672.69 thousand acres in 1980-81.The production of coconut declined from 6123.7 million nuts in 1971-72 to 5677.4 million nuts in 1980-81.This was due to wilt attack (root disease) in Kerala. Though there was general decline in the all India production per hectare from 5626 nuts per hectare in 1970-71 to 5249 nuts in 1980-81, the productivity in Karnataka showed a steady increase from 4838 nuts to 5178 nuts per hectare. But the average palm yield in Karnataka is 54 nuts and the yield per hectare is lower because of lower palm density. The researcher concludes his study with his findings that the farmers are not yet convinced about the advantages of hybrid varieties. They are also not aware of the improved methods of coconut cultivation. Gupta suggests the following steps to promote coconut culture (1) Establishment of state-owned nurseries in taluks with population above 20,000. (2) The Horticulture

Department should undertake vigorous campaign to educate the coconut farmers in improved methods of coconut cultivation. (3) Coconut farmers should adopt recommended 'package of practices'. (4) Overcrowding of palms in the existing gardens should be discouraged. [16]

K. Ganesamoorthy, C. Narayanan, D. Packiaraj, S. Rajarethinam and H. H. Khan of the Coconut Research Station, Veppankulam, Thanjavur conducted an in-depth study on genetic improvement of coconut in Tamilnadu. According to them, collection, conservation and evaluation of germplasm of coconut is one of the prerequisites for the crop improvement programme. Systematic survey and collection of indigenous germplasm started by the Coconut Research Station, Kasargod as early as 1918 and followed up by the Aliyarnagar Research Station at Coimbatore resulted in the enrichment of coconut gene pool. The release of the first hybrid coconut VHC1 developed at Veppumkulam by the Tamilnadu Agricultural University in 1982 was an important landmark in the history of coconut breeding in Tamilnadu. A cross between East Coast Tall x Dwarf Green was found to be the most promising with a mean nut yield of 115 nuts/palm/year and 21648 nuts/ha. Encouraged by the superior performance of hybrids and their reciprocal combinations, different inter and intra varietal crosses involving promising exotic and indigenous varieties were made in all possible combinations viz: Tall x Tall, Tall x Dwarf, Dwarf x Tall and Dwarf x Dwarf at Veppomkulam. Moreover these researchers pin point the efforts made for breeding varieties, resistant to pests and diseases also. They conclude their study with a note that in a crop like coconut which has a long pre-bearing period and takes a long time to attain yield stability, genetic improvement by breeding is slow and time consuming. However significant progress has been made. Successful exploitation of hybrid vigour by the scientists of the Tamilnadu Agricultural University has resulted in the development and release of three high yielding hybrids viz: VHC1, VHC2 and VHC3 with high nut and copra yield.

Screening of coconut germ plasm for important pest and diseases viz: leaf blight, basal stem rot and eriophid mite has resulted in the identification of resistant tolerant types and are being used in the breeding programmes to evolve tolerant varieties.[17]

R. K. Sivanappan points out the wastage of scarce water in surface irrigation of coconut fields. In surface irrigation the entire field is flooded to a depth of 5 to 7 cm once in 5 to 10 days depending upon the type of soil. The quantity of water applied works out to more than 200 litres/day or about 1000-1400 litres in 5-7 days. The conveyance loss is about 20-25 per cent. In contrast to this method is the Drip/Micro Sprinkler Method which has increased water use efficiency and water saving is up to 40 to 60 per cent and labour saving up to 90 per cent. Further Drip Method increases the yield by 30 per cent. This method successfully meets the problem of irrigating sandy tracts. Many progressive farmers of Tamilnadu and Karnataka have adopted this advanced method of irrigation. Sivanappan feels that the time is not far away when the entire coconut farm in the country will be irrigated by Drip System for its sustainability and to increase yield. [18]

R. Venkitaswamy and H. Hameed Khan have dealt with Drought Management in coconut in Tamil Nadu and point out that drought management is the foremost requirement in the western districts of Tamilnadu viz: Coimbatore, Erode and Dindugal. They suggest economic utilization of available irrigation water and adoption of the soil moisture conservation practices for containing drought. Methods recommended are: crop irrigation equal to 100 per cent or 66 per cent of pan evaporation or basin irrigation with 1W/CPE ratio of 1.0 at 4 cm depth and adoption of soil moisture conservation method like surface mulching with raw coir pith, coconut leaves or husks and husk burial.[19]

M. J. Prabhu says that coconut yield is comparatively low especially in coastal area. Referring to the experiment conducted by the Central Plantation Crops Research Institute,

Kasargod, Kerala, Prabhu points out that the reason for the poor nut yield is the poor sandy soils, poor retentive capacity for water and nutrients.

One of the methods to increase nut production is growing different grass varieties in coconut garden using husk and coir pith. Coir pith and husk have high water holding capacity of 5-6 times their weight. Their use increases the water holding capacity by about 40 percent. Husk and coir pith are placed in trenches of about 30x30cm to a height of 5 cm and filled with sand. Hybrid grass varieties such as bajira, napier and Co 3 are planted 50x50 cm apart. Application of farm yard manure and vermicompost at the rate of 5 tonnes per hectare for the coconut trees and fertilizer application of about 50 kg urea, 40 kg phosphorus and 40kg potash at the time of planting grass are recommended. Sprinkler irrigation once in 3-4 days result in harvesting grass after 80 days, subsequent cuttings at 45-50 days interval, thus growing about 100 tonnes of green fodder from one location which is sufficient to maintain a dairy unit of about 6-8 mulch cattle fetching a net income of ₹ 75000 to 1,00,000 every year. Husk and pith technology also has the advantage of acting as a natural barrier against entry of sea water in times of natural calamities such as 'tsunami', because the intercropped coconut trees along the coastal belt are able to withstand the saline concentration and water-logging compared with other trees in the coastal regions. [20]

Srikumar Poduval gives out a list of technologies available with the Coconut Development Board for assisting the entrepreneurs in the preparation of project reports for promoting coconut based industries. The Board's special attention is to develop small scale cottage industries in the coconut processing sector by providing technical and financial assistance in the form of subsidies and soft loans under the buy-back arrangements. Sreekumar emphasizes that the medium and large industries should come forward to encourage small scale units and assist them in areas like technology transfer, finance and expertise. Further the Research and Development in the coconut processing sector should concentrate its attention on the development of appropriate technology in coconut processing to the advantage of farmers, small scale processors and for regional development. Moreover research collaboration between coconut researchers both within India and other coconut producing countries should be maintained and the possibility of establishing a network within the country and amongst other coconut producing countries should be explored so as to exchange information on various technologies for mutual benefit.[21]

M.K.Nair and M.K.Rajesh give a clear exposition of coconut area, production and productivity in the country and attribute the following factors for increasing production and productivity: (1) High yielding varieties and hybrids; (2) Manures and fertilizers; (3) Irrigation; (4) inter cultivation; and (5) pest and disease management. They also point out the major production constraints viz : (1) the wide gap between demand and supply of quality seedlings; (2) smallness of holdings where the farmer raises other crops for meeting his requirements viz: nuts, fruits, vegetables, tubers and even fuel and the consequent neglect of coconut; (3) overcrowding of palms; (4) Insufficient and improper application of manure; (5) Irrigation constraints. These researches suggest the following strategies for improving production and productivity: (1)establishing seeds garden to produce seedlings of already proven high-yielding varieties/hybrids; (2) Identifying varieties suitable for different agro-climatic conditions; (3) Evolving hybrids and varieties tolerant to important diseases; (4) Developing location specific fertilizer and irrigation taking into consideration soil characteristics, rainfall distribution, temperature, relative humidity, nutrient status, ground water level etc.; and (5) Effort should be continued to design the already developed pest management technologies to reduce crop loss.[22]

P.S. Surendira Kumar, et al., have conducted experimental study on intercropping in coconut and point out its advantages. Though the contribution of Tamilnadu to the total area under coconut in the country steadily increased, productivity of coconut plantation on monocrop in the state is not so remunerative. Since the coconut trees are spaced at 7.5x7.5 meters and the active root zone of a palm is confined to a radius of 2 metres i.e. 25 per cent of the land surface laterally, the remaining 75 per cent of the land area can be used efficiently by raising intercrop such as food crops like banana, cereals, legumes and fruits, cash crops like black pepper, cocoa, cinnamon, cloves, coffee and nutmeg, cut flowers like anthurium and orchids as well as pasture crops, spices and condiments. The spices preferred are banana, pepper, coffee, ginger, turmeric, vegetables and pineapple, as these can be grown successfully under shade and they provide a good income to the farmers. According to these researchers, among the different cropping systems tried, coconut+ yam is superior, the annual yield per hectare under the system being 16625 nuts and 11033 kgs of yam. Maximum net profit is ₹ 29687 due to less input application for yam. This was followed by coconut + banana. Mixed farming in coconut gardens creates congenial conditions for the rapid multiplication of micro organisms in the soil. Continuous additions of plant residues by the component crops and the organic recycling facilitated by intercropping exert a facilitated development influence on the microbial population in the rhizosphere and it might influence the nutrition uptake of different crops. Surendirakumar, et al, conclude with an emphasis that coconut +yam increases the return by 35 per cent and hence it is a viable agro technique to improve the farm productivity.[23]

According to C. Natarajan, et al, all the hybrids developed in the Coconut Research Station at Veppankulam in Tamilnadu is superior in yield performance. This variety has been developed through cross pollination between well adopted local ecotypes East Coast Tall (ECT) as ovule parent and

Malaysian Orange Dwarf (MOD) as pollen parent. The performance of ECTxMOD in comparison with VHC2 on hectare basis shows that the former recorded 22570 nuts/ hectare as against 20950 nuts in VHC 2. The analysis of nut components indicated that the copra content of VHC 3 is 162g/ nut as against 146g in VHC 2. The new hybrid also gave a high oil yield of 2.55 tones/hectare.[24]

K.M.Pandalai describes the wide adaptability of the coconut palm which can tolerate a very wide range of soil and climatic conditions. Though the palm is described as essentially a native of the tropics, thriving well within 23° north and south latitudes and upto an altitude of about 3000 feet above sea level, it is a sea-side palm flourishing in a sea washed well drained coast with constant moving water in the soil in an atmosphere of saline moisture. The palm has been found to grow in a variety of soil types-white or gravelly sand, alluvial soils, literate soils, peaty or kary soils, estuarine deposits, lime-stone derived soils, volcanic pumice soils, marine, granite and coral soils. The best soil, however, appears to be a rich alluvium/or loam having proper soil moisture and drainage as found in the backwater areas of Travancore, Cochin, Malabar and the deltaic tracks of the Godavary. Coconut palms come up well in sandy soils especially of the littoral type, provided there is an assured supply of good underground water within easy reach of the roots and proper manuring.[25]

Mohan Rajesh attributes poor yield of coconut and the consequent frustration of the coconut farmers to lack of proper agricultural management practices. He suggests the following steps to increase the income from coconut plantation:

(*a*) Removal of unwanted trees which interfere with the main crop of coconut.

(*b*) Keep only the healthy and vigorous potential palms.

(*c*) Collect and burn all decaying matters to get rid of black beetles and red weevils which are the most harmful coconut pests.

(*d*) Conserve soil and build it up with bunds and required drains with silt pits along the leader drains so as to avoid soil erosion.

(*e*) Conserve moisture by avoiding outflow of rain water from the coconut farm as far as possible without water logging. This will increase nut formation and reduce premature nut fall.

(*f*) In order to conserve moisture and thereby avoid stresses to the palms during dry periods, coconut husk can be buried in the field itself.

(*g*) Grow green manure trees like Gliricidia along the borders, sides of internal roads and if possible between coconut rows. Further, creepers such as puraria and vitiver grass can be grown on bunds. Prune these before hardening and put at palm base. This practice helps to loosen the soil to absorb more water during rains and increase the bio-mass content, microbes and earth worm population and thereby enhances soil fertility and reduces costly artificial fertilizers.

(*h*) Since coconut does not perish in short periods and can be kept for about two months, producers have some staying power and so they can afford to wait for higher prices.

(*i*) Coconuts can be offered for sale in different markets as curry nuts, copra and for fresh nut export. Hence the farmers should choose the market in accordance with the possibilities for getting higher prices for their produce.[26]

George V.Thomas, et al, of the Central Plantation Crops Research Institute, Kasargod have dealt with production Technology for sustainable coconut cultivation. Pointing out the fact that the low production of coconut in India i.e around 40 nuts/palm/year is due to lack of adoption of scientific cultivation practices that can enhance productivity, they hold that application of low cost production technologies in the right combination suitable for coconut cultivation can help to enhance productivity. Integrated approach in nutrient management by way of recycling crop biomass, raising green manure legumes and green leaf manure plants and their incorporation and the use of bio fertilizers are some of the efficient low cost production technologies. Biological management of soil fertility in coconut plantation is cost effective, environment friendly, easily adoptable and makes efficient utilization of local resources. Soil and water conservation structures are vital to conserve natural resources for enhanced productivity.[27]

M. Lathika and C.E. Ajithkumar examined the growth trends in coconut area, production and productivity for five years (2000-2005) in the different coconut producing states of India and came to the conclusion that area effect assumes greater role in output growth in almost all coconut regions of the country, though some states like Kerala and Orissa recently showed signs of a productivity based output growth. States like Andhra Pradesh and Karnataka are already on the path of vast area expansion. But with severe pressures on land, the states of Kerala, Tamilnadu, Andamans and Nicobar Islands have registered only retarded growth in area. According to these researchers, avenues of replanting or dense —planting of coconut palms should be explored vigorously in some of the traditionally coconut growing states like Goa, Andaman and Nicobar Islands where the current yield level is abysmally low with practically no growth in the second phase i.e. 1996 to 2002. They conclude that area expansion of the crop is still a viable option for certain regions of the country. Yet the problem of growth stability in yield had been trickier to tackle with than the problem of stability in area growth and it warrants urgent attention.[28]

Marketing of Coconut

P. Rethinam, Executive Director, Asia and Pacific Coconut

Community (APCC), in his study on 'Steps for Yield Increase' says that nearly 50 products of coconut are being traded from the producing countries. Of them coconut oil is the largest coconut product. A critical look at the international trade reveals the fact that India has been an importer of all the major coconut products like copra, coconut oil, copra meal, desiccated coconut meta de coco and the like for meeting the domestic requirements. India is the largest single market for coconut. In 2003 India consumed more than her entire production of 12.9 billion nuts and domestic consumption exceeded production by 2.5 per cent. The price trend of copra, and coconut oil in India, Indonesia, the Philippines and Sri Lanka during 2001-2005 reveals that domestic prices are the highest in India and Sri Lanka and the lowest in Indonesia. Hence it is difficult for India to compete with other countries in the international market. This necessitates reduction in unit cost of production. However in view of the fact that every country is looking forward to India for marketing their products, the Indian Coconut farmer can definitely play a competitive role only if he takes up integrated coconut development with proper replanting and under planting, farm level processing linked with market and for a partnership with the private and public sectors.[29]

According to P. Rethinam India's share in the export of coir and coir products is sizeable whereas the export of other coconut based products is very negligible. Increasing global population and demand for coconut products, changing consumer preferences, intensifying safety and security concerns and shifting marketing networks have significant impact on the character and shape of the global market for coconut products.

At the same time critical developments like substitutes and increasing volatility of prices are a threat to the future of the coconut industry. Still increasing population world over and decreasing demand for coconut products widens the scope for increasing India's competitiveness provided productivity is increased and production cost is reduced, besides maintaining quality standards at international standard. According to Rethinam, of all the coconut based industries like copra making, oil making, cream making, milk powder making, desiccated coconut making, making coconut water concentrate and jam, vinegar, coconut water packing etc only oil and copra making dominate and their marketing only decides the price of the coconut.

The researcher concludes his study by pointing out the need for a more intensified approach in marketing strategy. Besides the efforts of the Coconut Development Board and the Government of India to popularize coconut water as a health drink, it is necessary that India should participate in international exhibitions and exhibit Indian coconut products for which the Gulf countries offer great opportunities.[30]

K. P. Ganesan points out that after the removal of restriction on the import of 715 items, India faces stiff competition in coconut and coconut oil from the Philippines and Indonesia.[31]

P.C. Maheswari, et. al, in their study on 'Marketing Strategies for Coconut' point out that, inspite of the fact India accounts for 25.57 per cent of the world production of coconut, the present system of marketing of coconut and its products is by and large unscientific and unorganized and is almost lacking in vertical integration. Coconut is a notified commodity. Still the absence of an efficient marketing system provides sufficient opportunities for middlemen to exploit the market. In almost all primary markets, they normally dictate the prices. Further there are several malpractices in the coconut market. Apart from this, during the past two decades there had been abnormal price fluctuation—both seasonal and cyclical. According to these researchers the chief marketing problems are:

(1) Farmers are unaware of the current market price of coconut. They are unable to understand the

methodology involved in fixing the price based on recovery percentage.

(2) Farmers do not have proper storing facilities to keep their produce until higher prices prevail in the market during lean seasons.

(3) Import of palm oil and vegetable oil from abroad tells heavily on the prospects of coconut cultivators and oil millers.

(4) Credit purchase of coconut by merchants from the garden itself and irregular and delayed payments of the low prices already fixed deprive the producer of his right to get fair prices.

(5) Though coconut is a notified product, it is not marketed through regulated markets.

These researchers suggest the following promotional activities: 1) Improving quality for export promotion; (2) Reduction of cost of production; (3) Product diversification and by product utilization. Diversification should be done at the farm level itself; (4) Formation of Coconut Committees in each Block consisting of representatives from the Agricultural Department, Coconut Board and growers to discuss coconut production and marketing problems; (5) To achieve market promotion and consumer awareness, extension programmes should be carried out by conducting trade fares and exhibitions; (6) Cooperative marketing; (7) Restriction of import of Copra and edible oils; (8) Revival of future trading; (9) Integrated multi-cropping; (10) Establishment of display and sales outlets for the processed products; and (11) Establishment of Coconut Technological Development Centres in the main coconut growing areas.[32]

C. Chandran's intensive study on 'Coconut Marketing in Tamil Nadu' explains the marketing practices such as harvests, grading, packing, marketing channel and the like and throws much light on the marketing costs, margins, price spread, effect of variations in the consumer's price on the share of the producer seller and the retailer as well as in the efficiency of the market system. Besides analyzing the problem faced by the traders in coconut marketing, the researcher concludes his study saying that marketing efficiency is high due to fewer middlemen and low marketing margin and the producer's share is inversely related to consumer's price while the retailer's share is positively related to consumer's price.[33]

M. Linson Mark's study on Marketing of Coconuts in the Agasteeswaram Taluk of Kanyakumari District reveals that the prices which rule the coconut market do not reflect the changes in demand.[34]

N. Namasivayam and V. Richard Paul's study highlights price spread in the marketing of coconut in the Theni District of Tamil Nadu. As per their analysis the marketing cost incurred by producers per thousand nuts was maximum (₹ 630.18) in Channel II consisting of Producer Commission Agents—whole salers—Retailers—consumers, followed by ₹ 610.00 in Channal III ie. Producer—Wholesaler—Retailers—Consumers. No marketing cost was incurred by producers in channel I consisting of Producers—Pre-harvest Contractors—Commission Agents—wholesalers—Retailers—Consumers, because the marketing cost was met by the Pre-harvest Contractors. Commission Agents incurred no marketing cost because of their non-performance in the field of cutting, loading, counting, grading and transportation. It was also found that under Channel III, the producers realized the maximum share of 58.73 per cent in consumer's price. Their share in Channel II and Channel I was 58.32 per cent and 50.20 per cent respectively. Commission Agents got very meagre margin with a small effort. Wholesalers got 6.02 per cent in Channel III, 4.57 per cent in Channels I, and II respectively. The share of the retailers worked out to equal the cost of all channels. The study also revealed that the marketing efficiency was higher in Channel III followed by Channel II and Channel I. [35]

P. Kameswara Rao points out that coconut in Andhra Pradesh is marketed in three major forms viz: dry coconut, copra and coconut oil. The only market for these items in the state is Ambajipeta. Palakol in West Godavari is the centre for water coconut marketing. Nearly 40 per cent of the coconut produced is marketed as water coconut and 30 per cent as dry coconut. The rest is marketed either as copra or oil or as both based on market demand. But coconut trade is facing certain problems including high degree of price fluctuations. All types of marketing channels viz: farmer, middle men, wholesaler and retailer exist. The existing market committees are not working properly. Most of them lack minimum facilities like sufficient yards and godowns. They collect market cess without providing required facilities. The dry coconut is mostly exported to Rajasthan, Madhya Pradesh and Maharashtra. Even transport has become a major constraint. Upto the 80's 99 per cent of the trade utilized rail wagons for transport. Thereafter the railways stopped allotting wagons. Instead rackes were allotted. It is highly impossible to avail this facility because quantities have to be pooled over a long period to load one racke, which causes spoilage of the commodity. Therefore road transport is resorted to. It is not only costly but also causes hardships to the traders.[36]

G.L. Kaul has dealt with the global competitiveness of coconut industry. He points out that coconut as a traditional crop, particularly in the third world, has not received the benefit of improved management technologies and market promotion. He has analysed the magnitude of threats facing the coconut industry such as competition from other oil-seed crops, low profitability, fluctuating prices, miscoceptions about coconut oil as an edible oil and inconsistent supplies of coconut products. He suggests the following strategies for ensuring a better future for the coconut farmers : (i) Major efforts should be made to improve productivity in all the countries including the coconut producing states of India; (ii) Productivity improvement requires greater research efforts to develop high-yielding varieties/hybrid with large nut size and resistant to major maladies, besides being drought tolerant; (iii) Intensification of land-use in the coconut gardens; (iv) Bringing down the cost of production which needs urgent consideration; (v) Steps to reduce dependence on coconut oil as an edible oil and intensified efforts towards diversification for developing different products which are more profitable and (vi) Product development strategy would have to be supported by strong marketing support for expanding the demand through identification of new markets and undertaking a vigorous promotional campaign to counter the propaganda against consumption of coconut oil and products on health grounds. Kaul concludes that avenues are available to reduce the impact of the threat to the coconut industry. What is required is a strong political will, supported by major R&D efforts with a more open and strong global coordination to ensure a bright future for the coconut industry.[37]

In an exhaustive study of the current status of the coconut Industry, P.G. Punchideva says that one of the fears expressed in the sixties regarding the future of the coconut industry, apart from stagnation in production, was the restrictive nature of the market. However, product diversification and value addition brought in its train diversification of international coconut market too. Today more than 100 countries import coconut oil in big or small quantities. America and Europe still dominate the trade. Asian countries are increasingly getting into it and they emerge as a key importer of desiccated coconut. Apart from the traditional products, new products are finding their way to new markets.

Coconut shell charcoal is bought by more than thirty countries in the form of activated carbon, chief among them being U.K., France, Belgium, Holland, Japan, Korea, Taiwan, South Africa and Australia. There cannot be any country in the world where some part or derivative of coconut is not used in the daily life today, in the form of vegetable oil, margarine, beverage, bakery item, sweets, soap, shamboo, cosmetic, pharmaceuticals, carpets, rugs, hand crafts, brushes, mattresses furniture or as peat. Still competing substitutes pose a threat to coconut industry.[38]

Cost Efficiency

P.K. Thampan's study on the cost of raising and maintaining coconut plantation and the profitability of coconut farming reveals the fact that after meeting the initial expenditure on land, fencing, irrigation and buildings, in most places in Kerala the average expenditure over the first 7 years after planting tall variety palms is around ₹ 125,000 per hectare while the same in Tamil Nadu exceeds ₹ 175,000. The components which constitute maintenance cost are expenditure on manures and fertilizers, plant protection, cultural management, irrigation and harvesting. A Farm Household Survey involving 198 households ranging in farm size from 0.5 ha to 5 ha drawn from 10 panchayats representing the northern, middle and southern regions of Kerala, brought out the fact that the average quantity of organic manures used was 32.45 kg per palm per year and over the different size classes, the expenditure incurred on manures and fertilizers showed variation from ₹ 47.43 to ₹ 68.63 per palm per year, the average being ₹ 38.19 per palm per year. The next expenditure component is cultural management involving digging or ploughing, forming solid mounds and subsequent levelling. For this expenditure per palm is the highest at ₹ 44 for the size class below 0.5 ha and ₹ 40 for the size class above 5 ha. The amount spent for plant protection varied from ₹ 13 to ₹ 50 per palm per year, the lowest being in small holdings of less than 0.5 ha in size . In the state only less than 50 per cent of the holdings have irrigation facilities.In the study the per palm expenditure varied from ₹ 1.95 to ₹ 14.37 with the annual average for all size classes being ₹ 10.16. Harvesting cost is met in cash and kind. Cash part varies from ₹ 150 to ₹ 360 and kind part from 60 nuts to 4 nuts per 100 trees. At a price of

₹ 4 per nut and for an average 6 harvests per year the total expenditure ranged from ₹ 18 to 24 per palm per year.

The said survey's revelation is total maintenance cost increased progressively from ₹ 25,473 per ha for the lowest class below 0.5 ha to ₹ 28,190 per ha for the highest size class above 5 ha. An analysis of cost of production and income shows that the average household income from all the holdings worked out to ₹ 46,343.5 per ha. The highest household income is for size class 2-3 ha at ₹ 55,313 followed by class 1-2 ha at ₹ 50,969 and the lowest for the size class above 5 ha.

Thampan concludes his study pointing out that coconut farming in Kerala is generally profitable but the level of profitability showed substantial increase when intercropping with or without livestock, component is practised.[39]

M.K. Nair, C.V. Sairam and Gopalasundaram of the Central Plantation Crops Research Institute, Kasargod have conducted an indepth study of the possibilities of reducing the cost of production of coconut. According to them cost of production of coconut in India has increased considerably due to the steep rise in the factor costs, mainly of labour, fertilizers and transportation. The average cost of cultivating the palm in one hectare under rain-fed conditions with good management in Kerala ranges from ₹ 20750 during the first year to about ₹ 10500 between 6-7 years and to about ₹ 12000 between 8-60 years (at 1993-94 prices). But the average yield per palm is only 40. This low productivity and high cost results in low profit margin. Hence the researchers suggest this problem may be overcome through two approaches: (i) by reducing the annual cost of cultivation; and (ii) by reducing unit cost of production through higher productivity. Competitiveness in coconut production can be achieved by using non-monetary/low cost inputs, improved management practices and by adopting coconut based farming systems as well as by using modern equipments like dryer for post harvest operations. Low productivity of coconut in India is due to the predominance of local cultivars which are generally late bearers and poor yielders compared to high yielding varieties / hybrids. Therefore it is preferable to invest in high yielding varieties which have a higher benefit cost ratio, pay back period and internal rate of return.[40]

K. Gopalan and M.S. Venkataraman classified the cost of cultivation of coconut as follows: (i) Cost of bringing up the palms to the stage of bearing; (ii) Cost of maintenance under the first category includes cost of land, seedlings, manuring, watering and fencing. The second category includes all agricultural operations, manuring and harvesting. [41]

M.V. George and P.I. Joseph carried out a study on 'Cost Benefit Analysis of Investment in tree crops and arrived at the cost of production of coconuts by taking into account both capital and current expenses as the opportunity cost of land.[42]

Problems of Coconut Cultivation

D. Chowdry in his study 'Problems and Prospects of Coconut Cultivation in Assam' pinpoints the following problems of coconut cultivation in Assam. First, there is lack of awareness of the farmers on recent developments related to crop improvement, crop protection, production and cropping system; Secondly, there is a lack of quality planting materials to the farmers; Thirdly, lack of proper management practices, as coconut is grown in a very uncared condition without applying fertilizer and irrigation; Fourthly, pest problems and diseases caused by fungi and phytoplasma result in different degrees of crop loss.[43]

Srinivasan reports that the productivity of the coconut crop is constrained by various stresses. Among them, the root (wilt) disease is the major problem in southern districts of Kerala and Tamil Nadu and also in Goa. Srinivasan also reports that the root (wilt) affected palms are also affected by leaf rot. Incidence of leaf rot increases with increase in the incidence of root disease (wilt).[44]

Srinivasan and Gunasekaran have assessed the nature of the leaf rot disease. Leaf rot disease is considered as one of the devastating problems. They have assessed the quantitative pattern of fungal association and species composition of the disease. Srinivasan also found that the black rat, rattus tinn, is an important rodent pest of coconut in most of Lakshadweep Islands. It damages 35-50 per cent of the standing crops.[45]

Desai and others point out that coconut palm is attacked by 107 pests. Among them the leaf eating caterpillar is one of the major pests. It infests the coconut palm throughout the year with varying intensities. Under varying conditions sporadic outbreaks lead to severe damage. A peak infestation occurs during the months of February to May, which may even prolong to June in case of delayed monsoons.

Caterpillar lives on the lower surface of leaflets in galleries and feeds on chlorophyll. Dry and green patches which appear on the lower surface of the leaves are the major symptoms of infestation. Palms of all ages are susceptible to infestation by black headed caterpillar.[46]

REFERENCES

1. Raj Kumar S. and Thamilselvan, R. 'Importance of Coconut Cultivation', *Kisan World*, Vol. 32, No. 5,May 2005, p. 58.
2. Sugata Ghose, 'Coconut—India's Pride', *Kisan World*, Vol. 25, No. 8, August 1998, pp. 27-31.
3. Nagarajan S. S. 'Improving Coconut Farm Productivity with Silt', *Kisan World*, Vol. 25, No. 5, May 1998, pp.19-20.
4. Sugata Ghose, 'Progress in Coconut', *Kisan World*, Vol. 27, No. 5, May 2000, pp. 34-35.
5. Jose Mathew, 'Drip Irrigation—'A Successful Technology with Multiple Benefits', *Kisan World*, Vol. 30, No. 1, January, 2003, p. 50.
6. Veeraputhiran R. "Drip Irrigation for Sustainable Water Management', *Kisan World*, Vol. 32, No. 1, January 2005, pp. 49-51.

7. Sivanappan R. K. 'An Overview of Irrigation Methods', *Kisan World*, Vol. 32, No. 7, July 2005, pp. 46-47.

8. Rajagopal V., Arul Raj S., Sairam C. V. 'Coconut Industry—Improving Genetic Produce' *The Hindu, Survey of Indian Agriculture*, 2004, pp. 67-69.

9. Rethinam P. 'Coconut—Making Industry Competitive', *The Hindu, Survey of Indian Agriculture*, 2004, pp. 70-72.

10. Sugata Ghose, 'Coconut—Production—A New Look, *Kisan World*, Vol. 20, No. 11, November 1993, p. 52.

11. Christopher Lourduraj A. and Mylswamy V. "Coconut to Increase Productivity', *Kisan World*, Vol. 24, No.1, January 1997, p.54.

12. Halli R. 'New Horizons in Coconut Productivity', *Kisan World*, Vol. 23, No. 3 March 1996, pp. 38-39.

13. Iyer R.P. et. al, 'Super Yielder in Coconut', *Indian Farming*, 1979, pp.3-5.

14. Parameswara Gupta E.A. 'Processing and Consumption of Coconut in India', *Southern Economist*, Vol.35, No 19, February 1, 1997, p.20.

15. Markose V.T 'Coconut—Assured Bright Future', *The Hindu, Survey of Indian Agriculture*, 2000, pp.89-92.

16. Parameswara Gupta E.A. 'Trend in Area, Production and Productivity of Coconut in India. A Study of Karnataka', *Southern Economist*, Vol.35, No.15&16, December 1-15, 1996, pp 26-28.

17. GanesaMoorthy K., Narayanan C., Packiaraj P., Rajarathinam S. and Khan H.H. 'Genetic Improvement in Coconut in Tamilnadu', *Indian Coconut Journal*, Volume XXIV, No.1, May, 2003, pp.9-12.

18. Sivanappan R.K. 'Drip Irrigation for Coconut for Increased Yield', *Kisan World*, Vol. 31, No. 10, October, 2004, pp.47-48.

19. Venkitaswamy R. and Hameed Khan H. 'Drought Management in coconut in Tamil nadu', *Indian Coconut Journal*, Vol. XXX1V, No.10. February 2004, pp. 16-18.

20. Prabhu M. J. '*Increasing Coconut Yield in Coastal Sand and Soils*', Farmers Note Book-The Hindu, March 30, p. 18.

21. Sreekumar Poduval, 'Technologies for Non-traditional Coconut Products', *Indian Coconut Journal*, May & June 1995, pp. 4-6.

22. Nair M.K. and Rajesh M.K. 'Coconut Production and Productivity', *Indian Coconut Journal*, Vol.XXXIII, No.2, June, 2001, pp.12-20.

23. Surendirakumar P.S., Kalyanasundaram D., Kavitha S. and Sampathkumar G. 'Inter Cropping in Coconut to Improve the Farm Productivity', *Indian Coconut Journal*, Vol. XXXIII, No.5, September 2005, pp. 13-14.

24. Natarajan C., Giridharan S. and Bhaskaran R. 'VHC 3-New Coconut Hybrid for Tamilnadu', *Indian Coconut Journal*, Vol.XXX1, No.9, January, 2001, pp. 10-11.

25. Pandalai K.M. 'Is Coconut Tract Bound?', *Indian Coconut Journal*, Vol. XXX, No.1, May 1999, pp.13-14.

26. Mohan Rajesh, 'Increased Income from Coconut Plantation', *Kisan World*, Vol.33, No.7, July 2006, pp. 53-54.

27. George V Thomas, Krishnakumar V., Dhanapal R., Murali Gopal and Alka Gupta, 'Production Technology for Sustainable Coconut Cultivation', *Indian Coconut Journal*, Vol. XXXVII, No.2, June, 2006, pp. 2-8.

28. Lathika and Ajithkumar C.E. 'Growth Trends in Area, Production and Productivity of Coconut in India', *Indian Journal of Agricultural Economics*, Vol.60, No.4, October—December, 2005, pp. 686-696.

29. Rethinam P. 'Coconut—Steps for Yield Increase', *The Hindu Survey of Indian Agriculture*', 2005, pp. 89-92.

30. Rethinam P. 'Coconut – Making Industry Competitive', *The Hindu Survey of Indian Agriculture*, 2004, pp. 70-72.

31. Ganesan K.P. 'Coconut Farming – An Innovative Approach', *Kisan World*, Vol.28, No.8, August 2001, p. 53.

32. Maheshwari P.C., Rathika R., Edwin Ganadhas M. 'Marketing Strategies for Coconut', *Indian Journal of Marketing*, Vol. XXXIII, No.3, March 2003, pp. 10-12.

33. Chandran C. 'A Study, of Coconut Marketing in Tamil Nadu', Ph.D. Thesis, M.K. University, Madurai, 1992.

34. Linson Mark M. 'Marketing of Coconuts in the Agasteeswaram Taluk of Kanyakumari District', M.Phil Dissertation, M.K. University, 1982.

35. Namasivayam N. & Richard Paul V. 'Price Spread in Marketing of Coconut in Tamil Nadu' *Indian Journal of Marketing*, Vol. XXXVI, No.7, July, 2006, pp. 3-5.

36. Kameswara Rao P. 'Coconut Marketing in Andhra Pradesh : Problems and Prospects', *Indian Coconut Journal*, Vol. XXVI, No.1&2, May & June,1995, pp. 18-19.

37. Kaul G.L. 'Global Competitiveness of Coconut Industry,' *Indian Coconut Journal*, Vol. XXVI, No.4, August 1995, pp. 2-5.

38. Punchideva P.G. 'Current Status of the Coconut Industry,' *Indian Coconut Journal*, Vol. XXXI, No.6, October 2000, pp. 1-12.

39. Thampan P.K. 'Profitability of Coconut Farming', *Kisan World*, Vol.26, No.10, October 1999, pp. 23-24.

40. Nair M.K. et.al., 'Competitiveness Through Cost Reduction and Higher Productivity in Coconut', *Indian Coconut Journal*, Vol. XXVI, No.4, August 1995, pp. 6-13.

41. Gopalan K. and Venkataraman M.S. 'Cost of Cultivation of Coconut in Travancore', *Indian Coconut Journal*, 1951, pp. 57-58.

42. George M.V. and Joseph P.I. 'Cost Benefit Analysis of Investment in Tree Crops', *Indian Journal of Agricultural Economics*, 1973, pp. 173-180.

43. Choudhury D. 2002, 'Problems and Prospects of Coconut Cultivation in Assam', *Indian Coconut Journal*, Vol.XXXII, No.10, February 2002, pp. 10-12.

44. Srinivasan N. 2002, 'Coconut Leaf Rot Complex and Perspectives for the Disease Control', *Indian Coconut Journal*, Vol. XXXII, No. 9, p. 2.

45. Srinivasan N. and Ganasekharam M. 1996, 'Pathogeniety of Preponderant Fungi Associated with Leaf rot Disease of Coconut', *Indian Coconut Journal*.

46. Desai V.S. *et.al*, 2003, 'Biological Control of Coconut', Black-headed caterpillar Opisina Arenosella W/K, *Indian Coconut Journal*, Vol. XXXIV, No. 7, p. 6.

Chapter 4 Coconut Production *(An Overview)*

Introduction

Coconut is cultivated in all parts of the world, for the simple reason that it grows even in temperate lands. It does not penetrate its root too deep. Coconut is a perishable commodity and it has long been used by the people in their day to day life in cooking, bathing and preparing medicines. It earns foreign exchange to those countries which produce coconut products and export them to the needy countries.

Coconut is produced in the American and African countries, the Asian countries, Pacific countries and the Asian Pacific Coconut Community (APCC) countries comprising India, Indonesia, Vietnam, Papua New Guinea, Philippines, Sri Lanka, Thailand and others.

Secondary data relating to world area under coconut cultivation, world production of coconuts, world productivity of coconuts, area under coconut cultivation in APCC countries, production of coconut in APCC countries, productivity of coconut in APCC countries and area under coconut cultivation, production of coconuts, productivity of coconuts in India, Tamil Nadu, Kanyakumari and different Taluks of Kanyakumari were collected and analysed by using statistical methods like averages, percentages, ranking, standard deviation and co-efficient of variation.

World Area under Coconut Cultivation

The world area under coconut cultivation during 1987-2006, in 1000 hectares is presented in Table 4.1.

Table 4.1. World Area under Coconut Cultivation during 1987-2006 (in 1000 hectares)

Year	APCC Countries	Asia	Pacific	Africa	America	Total
1987	9698	61	56	422	248	10385
1988	9806	62	56	434	264	10622
1989	9844	62	56	445	242	10649
1990	9991	65	53	451	227	10787
1991	10134	N.A.	N.A.	N.A.	N.A.	10934
1992	10105	63	93	444	484	11189
1993	10090	64	90	446	448	11138
1994	10272	65	90	466	456	11349
1995	10398	67	90	460	459	11474
1996	10486	65	91	460	476	11578
1997	10597	106	49	652	632	12036
1998	10536	97	56	660	567	11916
1999	10381	96	46	670	589	11782
2000	10357	98	44	656	599	11754
2001	10442	101	44	657	601	11845
2002	10678	105	60	650	629	12122
2003	10682	120	54	636	631	12123
2004	10652	117	53	649	649	12120
2005	10691	118	53	649	656	12167
2006	10482	120	53	627	512	11794
Total	**206222**	**1652**	**1187**	**10534**	**9369**	**229764**
Average	10311.1	82.6	59.35	526.7	468.45	11488.2
Per cent	89.75	0.72	0.52	4.58	4.08	100
Rank	1	4	5	2	3	

Source: Compiled from information provided by APCC Member Countries and Food and Agriculture Organization (FAO) year Books

NA—Not Available.

Table 4.1 presents the average world area under coconut cultivation from 1987 to 2006. Among the major countries of the world cultivating coconut, the APCC countries occupied the first rank, with an average of 10311.1 thousand hectares, followed by Africa ranking second with 526.7 thousand hectares, America ranking third with 468.45 thousand hectares, Asia ranking fourth with 82.6 thousand hectares and the Pacific countries in the fifth rank with 59.35 thousand hectares.

The APCC countries contributed 89.75 per cent share of the total area under coconut cultivation, followed by Africa with 4.58 per cent, America 4.08 per cent, and Asia 0.72 per cent and the Pacific 0.52 per cent during the period of study.

In 2005, the APCC countries had the highest area of 10,691 thousand hectares under coconut cultivation accounting for 87 per cent of the total area of 12167 thousand hectares under cultivation in the world, due to the invariable spread of rain in the countries.

In 1999, the African countries had the highest area of 670 thousand hectares under coconut cultivation accounting for 5.7 per cent of the total world area under cultivation which was 11,782 thousand hectares, due to the scarcity of rain in the countries.

In 2005, the American countries had the highest area of 656 thousand hectares under coconut cultivation accounting for 5.4 per cent of the total world area of 12167 thousand hectares under cultivation due to the low spread of rain in the countries.

In 1987, the APCC countries had the largest area of 9598 thousand hectares under coconut cultivation accounting for 92.4 per cent of the total world area under cultivation which was 10,385 thousand hectares due to the uneven spread of rain in the countries.

In 2000, the Pacific countries had the smallest area of 44 thousand hectares under coconut cultivation accounting for 0.4 per cent of the total world area under cultivation which was 11,754 thousand hectares, due to the non spread of rain in the countries.

In 1990, the American countries had the smallest area of 227 thousand hectares under coconut cultivation accounting for 2.1 per cent of the total world area of 10787 thousand hectares under cultivation due to failure of monsoon in the countries.

Compound Growth Rate and Magnitude of Variability

The annual compound growth rates of area under coconut cultivation among the world countries during 1987-2006 and their magnitude of variability are furnished in Table 4.2.

Table 4.2. Trend Coefficient, Growth Rate and Magnitude of Variability of Area under Coconut Cultivation among the World Countries during 1987-2006

Countries	Semi-log		R^2	CGR (Per cent/ Annum)	CV (Per cent)
	Constant	Regression Co-efficient			
APCC Countries	9.190 (0.007)	0.00477** (0.001)	0.803	1.13	3.12
Asia	3.965 (0.052)	0.0431** (0.004)	0.856	10.43	28.68
Pacific	4.268 (0.124)	-0.0156 NS (0.010)	0.123	-3.66	30.14
Africa	5.994 (0.48)	0.0284** (0.004)	0.755	6.76	19.92
America	5.576 (0.094)	0.0527** (0.008)	0.733	12.93	31.7
Total	9.265 (0.009)	0.00793** (0.001)	0.861	1.84	4.99

Source: Computed Data

**Significant at one per cent level

NS—Not Significant.

Growth Rate

It could be seen from Table 4.2 that the area under coconut cultivation among the world countries increased at the rate of 1.84 per cent per annum. It has also been observed that the trend coefficient is positive in all countries except the Pacific and significant at one per cent level indicating an increasing trend in the area under coconut cultivation among the countries of the world during 1987-2006.

It is also inferred from the Table that among the countries of the world, the area under coconut cultivation in the American countries had increased at the rate of 12.93 per cent per annum followed by 10.43 per cent per annum in the Asian countries, 6.76 per cent per annum in the African countries and 1.13 per cent per annum in the APCC countries. The area under coconut cultivation had decreased at the rate of 3.66 per cent per annum in the case of the Pacific countries.

Magnitude of Variability

It is also seen from Table 4.2 that the area under coconut cultivation in the American countries had experienced a variation of 31.7 per cent followed by a variation of 30.14 per cent in the Pacific, 28.68 per cent in the Asia, 19.92 per cent in Africa and 3.12 per cent in the APCC countries. On the whole, the rate of variation in coconut cultivation in the world countries during the period of study was 4.99 per cent.

World Production of Coconuts

The world production of coconut during 1987-2006, in 1000s is presented in Table 4.3 *(See on next page)*.

Table 4.3 presents the average world production of coconuts from 1987 to 2006. Among the major countries in the world producing of coconuts, the APCC countries occupy the first rank with 4,47,41,932.5 thousand nuts, followed by America occupying the second rank with 43,30,133.7 thousand nuts, Africa in the third rank with 22,71,757 thousand nuts, Asia in the fourth rank with 7,10,004.6 thousand nuts and the Pacific countries ranking fifth with 32,75,444.75 thousand nuts.

The APCC countries contributed 85.42 per cent share of the total world production of coconuts followed by America's share of 8.27 per cent, Africa's 4.34 per cent, Asia's 1.36 per cent and the Pacific's share of 0.63 per cent during the period of study.

Table 4.3. World Production of Coconuts during 1987-2006

(in 1000 nuts)

Year	APCC Countries	Asia	Pacific	Africa	America	Total
1987	37101800	678750	378750	2353750	3296250	43809300
1988	37044200	538750	406250	2405000	3641250	44035450
1989	38812600	493750	333750	2442500	3581250	45663850
1990	40349000	493750	316250	2477500	3608750	47245250
1991	39512000	465000	345000	2535000	3735000	46622000
1992	41149000	634430	330375	2129145	3352218	47595168
1993	42785000	564834	321875	2230674	3097368	48999750
1994	44557200	585011	320000	2181004	3487416	51130631
1995	47391040	583219	321625	2196295	3522878	54015056
1996	47021000	587875	325750	2193000	3469929	53597554
1997	47796320	611476	245000	2277798	3509284	54439878
1998	46696500	706049	242500	2303813	3560436	53509298
1999	46707500	754728	271729	2342875	4723786	54800618
2000	48201500	750766	271106	2187625	5088071	56499069
2001	47886170	756663	271106	2187625	5288873	56390436
2002	48674350	910644	371606	2170450	5977589	58104638
2003	48819700	1009685	369250	2187075	6041117	58426827
2004	47663159	1045412	368625	2200700	6325253	57603149
2005	49620300	973071	368937	2200700	6406595	59569603
2006	47050311	1026228	371411	2232610	4889361	55569921
Total	**894838650**	**14200091**	**6550895**	**45435139**	**86602674**	**1047627446**
Average	44741932.5	710004.6	327544.75	2271757	4330133.7	52381372.3
Per cent	85.42	1.36	0.63	4.34	8.27	100
Rank	1	4	5	3	2	

Source: Compiled from information provided by APCC Member Countries and FAO Year Books.

In 2005, the APCC countries had the highest production of 4,96,20,300 thousand nuts accounting for 83.2 per cent of the total world production of coconuts which was 5,95,69,603 thousand nuts, due to the invariable spread of rain in the countries.

In 1991, the African countries had the highest production of 25,35,000 thousand nuts accounting for 5.43 per cent of the total world production of coconuts which was 4,66,22,000 thousand nuts, due to the spread of rain in the countries.

In 2005, the American countries had the highest production of 64,06,595 thousand nuts accounting for 10.7 per cent of the total world production of coconuts which was 5,95,69,603 thousand nuts, due to the spread of rain in the countries.

In 1988, the APCC countries had the smallest production of 3,70,44,200 thousand nuts accounting for 84 per cent of the total world production of coconuts which was 44,035,450 thousand nuts due to the uneven spread of rain in the countries. In 1991 the Asian countries had the smallest production of 4,65,000 thousand nuts accounting for 0.997 per cent of the total production of coconuts, which was 4,66,22,000 thousand nuts, due to the insufficient rain throughout the countries in the world.

In 1998, the Pacific countries had the smallest production of 2,42,500 thousand nuts, accounting for 0.45 per cent of the total world production of coconuts, which was 5,35,09,298 thousand nuts, due to the low rate of rain fall in the countries. In 1992, the African countries had the smallest production of 21,29,145 thousand nuts accounting for 4.5 per cent of the total world production of coconuts which was 4,75,95,168 thousand nuts.

Compound Growth Rate and Magnitude of Variability

The annual compound growth rates of world production of coconuts among the world countries during 1987-2006 and their magnitude of variability are furnished in Table 4.4 *(see on next page).*

Table 4.4. Trend Coefficient, Growth Rate and Magnitude of Variability in the Production of Coconuts among the World Countries during 1987-2006

Countries	Semi-log Constant	Semi-log Regression Co-efficient	R^2	C G R (Per cent/ Annum)	CV (Per cent)
APCC Countries	17.456 (0.021)	0.0148** (0.002)	0.807	3.47	9.41
Asia	13.042 (0.057)	0.0380** (0.005)	0.781	9.17	26.46
Pacific	12.710 (0.071)	0.000197 NS (0.006)	0.006	0.45	14.35
Africa	14.688 (0.019)	-0.0051 ** (0.002)	0.360	-1.18	5.12
America	14.882 (0.066)	0.0350** (0.005)	0.695	8.42	26.34
Total	**17.602 (0.015)**	**0.0159 ** (0.001)**	**0.901**	**3.73**	**9.70**

Source: Computed Data
**Significant at one per cent level
NS—Not Significant.

Growth Rate

It could be seen from Table 4.4 that the world production of coconuts among the world countries increased at the rate of 3.73 per cent per annum. It has also been observed from the table, that the trend coefficient is positive in all countries except in Africa and significant at one per cent level indicating an increasing trend in the world production of coconuts, among the countries of the world during 1987-2006.

It is also inferred from the above Table that among the countries of the world, the production of coconuts in the Asian countries had increased at the rate of 9.17 per cent per annum followed by 8.42 per cent per annum in the American countries, 3.47 per cent per annum in the APCC countries and 0.45 per cent per annum in the Pacific countries. It has decreased at the rate of 1.18 per cent per annum in African countries.

Magnitude of Variability

It is also seen from Table 4.4, that the production of coconuts in the APCC countries had experienced a variation of 9.41 per cent. There was also a variation of 26.46 per cent in Asia, 14.35 per cent in the Pacific, 5.12 per cent in Africa and 26.34 per cent in the American countries, in the world production of coconuts. On the whole, the rate of variation in coconut cultivation in the world countries during the period of study was 9.70 per cent.

World Productivity of Coconuts

The world productivity of coconuts during 1987-2006, (in nuts per hectare) is presented in Table 4.5.

Table 4.5. World Productivity of Coconuts during 1987-2006

(in nuts per hectare)

Year	APCC Countries	Asia	Pacifics	Africa	America
1987	3865.58	11127.05	6763.,39	5577.61	13291.33
1988	3777.71	8689.52	7254.46	5541.47	13792.61
1989	3942.77	7963.71	5959.82	5488.76	14798.55
1990	4038.53	7596.15	5966.98	5493.35	15897.58
1991	3898.95	N.A.	N.A.	N.A.	N.A.
1992	4072.14	10070.32	3552.42	4795.37	6926.07
1993	4240.34	8825.53	3576.39	5001.51	6913.77
1994	4337.73	9000.17	3555.56	4680.27	7647.84
1995	4557.71	8704.76	3573.61	4774.55	7675.12
1996	4484.17	9044.23	3579.67	4767.39	7289.77
1997	4510.36	5768.64	5000.00	3493.56	5552.56
1998	4432.09	7278.86	4330.36	3490.63	6279.43
1999	4499.33	7861.75	5907.15	3496.83	8020.01
2000	4654.00	7660.88	6161.5	3334.79	8494.28
2001	4585.92	7491.71	6161.5	3329.72	8800.12
2002	4585.38	8672.8	6193.43	3339.15	9503.32
2003	4570.28	8414.04	6837.96	3438.8	9573.88
2004	4474.57	8935.15	6955.19	3390.91	9746.15
2005	4641.32	8246.36	6961.08	3390.91	9766.15
2006	4488.68	8551.9	7007.75	3560.78	9549.53
Average	4331.528	7995.177	5264.911	4019.318	8975.909
Rank	4	2	3	5	1

Source: Compiled from information provided by APCC Member Countries and FAO Year Books

Table 4.5 presents the average world productivity of coconuts from 1987 to 2006. Among the major countries, on world productivity of coconuts, America occupied the first rank with 8,975.909 nuts per hectare, followed by the Asian countries in the second rank, with 7,995.177 nuts per hectare, the Pacific in the third rank with 5,264.911 nuts per hectare, the APCC countries ranking fourth with 4,331.528 nuts per hectare and the African countries ranking fifth, with 4,019.318 nuts per hectare of the world productivity of coconuts.

In 2005, America had the highest productivity of 9,766.15 nuts per hectare, followed by Asia with 8,246 nuts per hectare, the Pacific with 6,961.08 nuts per hectare, the APCC countries with 4,641.32 nuts per hectare and Africa, with the lowest productivity of 3,390.91 nuts per hectare.

In 2000, Africa had the lowest productivity of 3,334.79 nuts per hectare followed by the APCC countries producing 4,654 nuts per hectare, the Pacific with 6,161.5 nuts per hectare, Asia with 7,660.88 nuts per hectare and America producing 8,494.28 nuts per hectare.

In 1995, Asia had the highest productivity of 8,704.76 nuts per hectare followed by America with 7,675.12 nuts, Africa with 4774.55 nuts, APCC countries 4,557.71 with nuts and the Pacific with the lowest productivity of 3,573.61 nuts per hectare.

In 1987, America had the highest productivity of 13,291.33 nuts per hectare, followed by Asia producing 11,127.05 nuts, the Pacific with 6,763.39 nuts, Africa with 5,577.61 nuts and the APCC countries with the lowest productivity of 3,865.58 nuts per hectare.

Compound Growth Rate of World Productivity and Magnitude of Variability

The annual compound growth rates of world productivity of coconuts, among the world countries during 1987-2006 and their magnitude of variability are furnished in Table 4.6.

Table 4.6. Trend Coefficient, Growth Rate and Magnitude of Variability in the Productivity of Coconuts among the World Countries during 1987-2006

Countries	Semi-log		R^2	CGR (Per cent/ Annum)	CV (Per cent)
	Constant	Regression Co-efficient			
APCC Countries	8.266 (0.016)	0.01007** (0.001)	0.757	2.34	6.67
Asia	9.095 (0.066)	- 0.0061 NS (0.005)	0.071	- 1.41	13.97
Pacific	8.434 (0.132)	0.01411 NS (0.011)	0.091	3.30	26.56
Africa	8.681 (0.043)	-0.0327 ** (0.004)	0.835	- 7.82	22.66
America	9.295 (0.138)	- 0.017 NS (0.011)	0.119	- 3.99	32.85
Total	**8.338 (0.010)**	**0.00799** (0.001)**	**0.833**	**1.85**	**5.14**

Source: Computed Data
**Significant at one per cent level
NS—Not Significant

Growth Rate

It could be seen from Table 4.6 that the productivity of coconuts among the world countries increased at the rate of 1.85 per cent per annum. It has also been observed from the Table that the trend coefficient is positive in countries except Africa, America, and Asia and significant at one per cent level indicating an increasing trend in the world productivity of coconuts among the countries of the world during 1987-2006.

It is also inferred from the Table that among the countries of the world, the productivity of coconuts had increased at the rate of 3.30 per cent per annum in the Pacific and the APCC countries. The productivity had decreased at the rate of 7.82 per cent per annum in the African countries, followed by 3.99 per cent per annum in the American countries and 1.41 per cent per annum in the Asian countries.

Magnitude of Variability

It is also seen from Table 4.6 that the productivity of coconuts in the APCC countries had experienced a variation of 6.67 per cent. There was also a variation of 13.97 per cent in Asia, 26.56 per cent in the Pacific, 22.66 per cent in Africa and 32.85 per cent in the American countries in world productivity of coconuts. On the whole, the rate of variation in the world countries during the period under study was 5.14 per cent.

Area under Coconut Cultivation in APCC Countries

APCC countries include India, Indonesia, Vietnam, Papua New Guinea, Phillipines, Sri Lanka, Thailand and others. Data relating to the area under coconut cultivation in APCC countries during 1987-2006, in 1000 hectares (Vide Annexure IV) were collected and compound growth rate and magnitude of variability were analysed.

Compound Growth Rate and Magnitude of Variability

The annual compound growth rates of area under coconut cultivation, among the countries of the APCC during 1987-2006 and their magnitude of variability are furnished in Table 4.7 *(See on next page)*.

Growth Rate

It could be seen from Table 4.7, that the area under coconut cultivation, among the APCC countries increased at the rate of 1.11 per cent per annum. It has also been observed from the Table that the trend coefficient is positive in all countries except Vietnam, Sri Lanka and Thailand and significant at one per cent level, indicating an increasing trend in the area under coconut cultivation, among the countries of the world during 1987-2006.

Table 4.7. Trend Coefficient, Growth Rate and Magnitude of Variability of Area under Coconut Cultivation among APCC Countries during 1987-2006

Countries	Semi–log		R^2	CGR (Per cent/ Annum)	CV (Per cent)
	Constant	Regression Co-efficient			
India	7.204 (0.024)	0.02124** (0.002)	0.864	5.01	12.84
Indonesia	8.098 (0.014)	0.00944** (0.001)	0.795	2.20	6.08
Vietnam	5.816 (0.053)	-0.0497** (0.004)	0.874	-12.21	33.32
Papua New Guinea	5.546 (0.007)	0.00108 NS (0.001)	0.143	0.25	1.64
Philippines	8.039 (0.009)	0.00139 NS (0.001)	0.147	0.32	2.15
Sri Lanka	6.053 (0.018)	- 0.00075 NS (0.001)	0.014	-0.17	3.71
Thailand	6.070 (0.044)	- 0.0176** (0.004)	0.562	-4.13	12.32
Total	**9.190 (0.007)**	**0.00478** (0.001)**	**0.803**	**1.11**	**3.12**

Source: Computed Data
**Significant at one per cent level
NS—Not Significant

It is also inferred from the Table that among the countries of the world, the area under coconut cultivation in India had increased at the rate of 5.01 per cent per annum, followed by 2.20 per cent per annum in Indonesia, 0.25 per cent per annum in Papua New Guinea and 0.32 per cent per annum in the Philippines. The area under coconut cultivation had decreased at the rate of 12.12 per cent per annum in Vietnam, 4.13 per cent per annum in Thailand and 0.17 per cent per annum in Sri Lanka during the study period.

Magnitude of Variability

It is also seen from the Table 4.7, that the variation in area under coconut cultivation in India had increased at the rate of 12.84 per cent. There was also a variation of 6.08 per cent in Indonesia, 33.32 per cent in Vietnam, 1.64 per cent in Papua New Guinea, 2.15 per cent in the Philippines, 3.71 per cent in Sri Lanka and 12.32 per cent in Thailand in the area under cultivation. On the whole, the rate of variation in coconut cultivation in the APCC countries during the period of study was 3.12 per cent.

Production of Coconuts in APCC Countries

Data related to the production of coconuts in APCC countries during 1987-2006, in 1000 nuts (Vide Annexure V) were collected and compound growth rate and magnitude of variability were analysed.

Compound Growth Rate and Magnitude of Variability

The annual compound growth rates of production of coconuts in APCC countries during 1987-2006 and their magnitude of variability are furnished in Table 4.8 *(See on next page)*.

Growth Rate

It could be seen from Table 4.8, that the production of coconuts among the APCC countries increased at the rate of 3.39 per cent per annum. It has also been observed that the trend coefficient is positive in all countries except Vietnam and Papua New Guinea and significant, indicating an increasing trend in the production of coconuts in the APCC countries during 1987-2006.

It is also inferred from the Table that among the APCC countries, the production of coconuts in India had increased at the rate of 6.64 per cent per annum, followed by 5.58 per cent per annum in Indonesia. 2.12 per cent per annum in Sri Lanka, 1.64 per cent per annum in Thailand and 1.53 per cent per annum in Philippines. The production of coconut had decreased at the rate of 2.49 per cent per annum in Vietnam and 6.09 per annum in Papua New Guinea.

Table 4.8. Trend Coefficient, Growth Rate and Magnitude of Variability in the Production of Coconuts among APCC Countries during 1987–2006

Countries	Semi–log		R^2	CGR (Per cent/ Annum)	CV (Per cent)
	Constant	Regression Co-efficient			
India	15.934 (0.064)	0.0279** (0.005)	0.600	6.64	18.58
Indonesia	16.173 (0.018)	0.0236** (0.002)	0.930	5.58	14.18
Vietnam	13.826 (0.099)	-0.0107NS (0.008)	0.850	-2.49	20.54
Papua New Guinea	13.948 (0.085)	-0.0257** (0.007)	0.418	-6.09	21.60
Philippines	16.273 (0.034)	0.00659* (0.003)	0.233	1.53	8.14
Sri Lanka	14.635 (0.046)	0.00909* (0.004)	0.234	2.12	10.95
Thailand	13.897 (0.091)	0.00705NS (0.008)	0.046	1.64	21.43
Total	**17.463 (0.022)**	**0.01449** (0.002)**	**0.773**	**3.39**	**9.34**

Source: Computed Data
*Significant at five per cent level
**Significant at one per cent level
NS—Not Significant

Magnitude of Variability

It is also seen from Table 4.8, that regarding the production of coconuts among the APCC countries, India had experienced a variation of 18.58 per cent. There was also a variation of

14.18 per cent in Indonesia, 20.54 per cent in Vietnam, 21.60 per cent in Papua New Guinea, 8.14 per cent in the Philippines, 10.95 per cent in Sri Lanka and 21.43 per cent in the Thailand in the production of coconut. On the whole the rate of variation in coconut production in the APCC countries during the period of study was 9.34 per cent.

Productivity of Coconuts in APCC Countries

The data relating to the productivity of coconuts in APCC countries during 1987-2006, in nuts per hectare (*Vide Annexure VI*) were collected and compound growth rate and magnitude of variability were analysed.

Compound Growth Rate and Magnitude of Variability

The annual compound growth rates of productivity of coconuts in the APCC countries during 1987-2006 and their magnitude of variability are furnished in Table 4.9 *(See on next page)*.

Growth Rate

It could be seen from Table 4.9, that the productivity of coconuts in the APCC countries, increased at the rate of 1.11 per cent per annum. It has also been observed from the table that the trend coefficient is positive in all countries except Papua New Guinea and Sri Lanka, indicating an increasing trend in the productivity of coconuts in APCC countries during 1987-2006.

It is also inferred from the Table 4.9, that among the APCC countries, the productivity of coconuts in Vietnam had increased at the rate of 9.40 per cent per annum followed by 5.83 per cent per annum by the Thailand, 3.32 per annum by Indonesia, 2.28 per cent per annum by Sri Lanka, 1.20 per cent by Philippines and 1.55 per cent per annum by India. The productivity had decreased by 6.34 per cent per annum in Papua New Guinea.

Table 4.9. Trend Coefficient, Growth Rate and Magnitude of Variability in the Productivity of Coconut Among APCC Countries during 1987–2006

Countries	Semi-log Constant	Semi-log Regression Co-efficient	R^2	CGR (Per cent/ Annum)	CV (Per cent)
India	8.730 (0.045)	0.0067^{NS} (0.004)	0.149	1.55	9.95
Indonesia	8.075 (0.015)	0.0142** (0.001)	0.881	3.32	9.00
Vietnam	8.010 (0.102)	0.039** (0.008)	0.541	9.40	25.73
Papua New Guinea	8.402 (0.087)	-0.0267** (0.007)	0.429	-6.34	22.67
Philippines	8.234 (0.029)	0.0052* (0.002)	0.200	1.20	6.94
Sri Lanka	8.581 (0.043)	0.0098* (0.004)	0.299	2.28	10.47
Thailand	7.827 (0.091)	0.0246** (0.008)	0.368	5.83	24.49
Total of APCC countries	**8.273 (0.018)**	**0.0097** (0.002)**	**0.690**	**2.26**	**6.71**

Source: Computed Data

* Significant at five per cent level

** Significant at one per cent level

NS—Not Significant

Magnitude of Variability

It is also seen from Table 4.9, that the productivity of coconuts in India had experienced a variation of 9.95 per cent. There was also a variation of 9 per cent in Indonesia, 25.73 per cent in Vietnam, 22.67 per cent in Papua New Guinea, 6.94 per cent in Philippines, 10.47 per cent in Sri Lanka and 24.49 per cent in Thailand in productivity. On the whole, the rate of variation in coconut productivity in the APCC countries during the period of study was 6.71 per cent.

Area Under Coconut Cultivation in India

The total area under coconut cultivation in India, increased significantly from the mid-eighties with little fluctuations. It got extended from 1231.1 hectares in 1986-87 to 1946.8 hectares in 2005-06. The area under coconut cultivation in India for the past twenty years is given in Table 4.10 *(See on next page)*. The table also shows the trend values and the percentage of increase or decrease in the area of coconut cultivation over the previous year.

From Table 4.10, it could be seen that the area under coconut cultivation in India, was the highest in 2005-06 and the lowest in 1988-87. The area under coconut cultivation had gone up from 1,231.1 hectares in 1986-87 to 1,946.8 hectares in 2005-06.

The area under coconut cultivation increased, remarkably; by 1,346 thousand hectares in 1987-88 and 1,830 thousand hectares in 1995-96, registering 9.32 per cent and 6.78 per cent increase respectively in the annual growth rate, over the previous years.

It is also observed from the table, that the area under coconut cultivation had gone down from 1,861 thousand hectares in 1997-98 to 1,754.5 thousand hectares in 1998-99, registering 5.72 per cent decrease over 1997-98, owing to severe incidence of wilt disease and unfavourable climatic conditions. Since, there was a substantial reduction in the area of cultivation in 2002-03 also, the production dropped. It is also found from the table, that trend value for area under coconut cultivation had increased from 1,364.111 hectares in 1986-87 to 2,036.819 hectares in 2005-06.

Table 4.10. Trend in Area under Coconut Cultivation in India from 1986-87 to 2005-06

Year	Area (1000 Ha)	Increase/ decrease	Percentage increase/ decrease	Trend value
1986-87	1231.1			1364.111
1987-88	1346	114.8	9.32	1399.517
1988-89	1425	79	5.87	1434.923
1989-90	1472.2	47.2	3.31	1470.328
1990-91	1513.9	41.7	2.83	1505.734
1991-92	1528.9	15	0.99	1541.14
1992-93	1537.7	8.8	0.58	1576.545
1993-94	1635.1	97.4	6.33	1611.951
1994-95	1713.8	78.7	4.81	1647.357
1995-96	1830	116.2	6.78	1682.762
1996-97	1890.8	60.8	3.32	1718.168
1997-98	1861	-29.8	-1.58	1753.573
1998-99	1754.5	-106.5	-5.72	1788.979
1999-00	1768.1	13.6	0.78	1824.385
2000-01	1839.8	71.7	4.06	1859.79
2001-02	1932.3	92.5	5.03	1895.196
2002-03	1913.5	-18.8	-0.97	1930.602
2003-04	1933.7	20.2	1.06	1966.007
2004-05	1935	1.3	0.07	2001.413
2005-06	1946.8	11.8	0.61	2036.819

Source: 1. Directorate of Economics and Statistics, Ministry of Agriculture, New Delhi.

2. Department of Economics and Statistics, Government of Kerala, Tiruvananthapuram.
3. Department of Statistics, Government of Tamil Nadu, Chennai.

Coconut Production in India

In India, coconut is an important small holder's plantation crop. It is grown in an area of 18.39 lakh hectares, mainly in the four southern states of Kerala, Tamil Nadu, Andhra Pradesh and Karnataka. In Kerala and parts of coastal Karnataka and Tamil Nadu, it is predominantly grown under rain-fed conditions and in the rest of the country it is grown under irrigated conditions. Small and marginal farmers, with an average holding size of less than 0.20 hectare in Kerala and 2 hectares in Karnataka, Tamil Nadu and Andhra Pradesh, predominate coconut production sector in the country.[1] On the whole, India accounts for 27.57 per cent of the world's coconut production.[2]

During the pre-independence period, Kerala confined regular coconut cultivation to the coastal tracts, and among the South Indian states was leading with 90 per cent share of the total production in the country.

The four southern states alone, occupy 90 per cent of the total coconut area, of which Kerala's share is nearly 60 per cent.[3] Coconut, an agricultural commodity, is cultivated invariably in all parts of the country. The trends in coconut production, area under coconut cultivation, the relative share of area under cultivation and productivity in relation to the states and the sample district during the period of study are discussed here.

Production of coconut in India, the absolute as well as percentage increase or decrease of coconut production over the previous years and the trend values are presented in Table 4.11.

From Table 4.11, it is observed that the production of coconut in India, ranged from a minimum of 6,376.8 million nuts in 1986-87 to a maximum of 14,811.1 million nuts in 2005-06. The production increased to 8,541.4 million nuts in 1988-89, which was a 17.49 per cent increase in the annual growth rate over the previous year. Expansion of area under

Table 4.11. Trend in Coconut Production in India from 1986-87 to 2005-06

Year	Production (million nuts)	Increase/ decrease	Percentage increase/ decrease	Trend value
1986-87	6376.8			8498.903
1987-88	7269.9	893.1	14.01	8808.288
1988-89	8541.4	1271.5	17.49	9117.674
1989-90	9358.8	817.4	9.57	9427.059
1990-91	9700.2	341.47	3.65	9736.445
1991-92	10079.6	379.4	3.91	10045.83
1992-93	11240.9	1161.3	11.52	10355.22
1993-94	11974.7	733.8	6.53	10664.6
1994-95	13299.6	1324.9	11.06	10973.99
1995-96	12952.3	-347.3	-2.61	11283.37
1996-97	13061	108.7	0.84	11592.76
1997-98	12717.3	-343.7	-2.63	11902.14
1998-99	12535.9	-181.4	-1.43	12211.53
1999-00	12129	-406.9	-3.25	12520.91
2000-01	12597.3	468.3	3.86	12830.3
2001-02	12963.2	365.9	2.90	13139.67
2002-03	12141.2	-822	-6.34	13449.07
2003-04	12178.2	37	0.30	13758.46
2004-05	12832.9	654.7	5.38	14067.84
2005-06	14811.1	1978.2	15.42	14377.23

Source: 1. Directorate of Economics and Statistics, Ministry of Agriculture, New Delhi.

2. Department of Economics and Statistics, Government of Kerala, Tiruvananthapuram.

3. Department of Statistics, Government of Tamil Nadu, Chennai.

cultivation to the tune of 79 hectares and congenial climatic conditions that prevailed contributed to the increase in coconut production.

The production of coconut, increased substantially to 13,299.6 million nuts in 1994-95 from 11,974.7 million nuts in 1993-94, registering 11.06 per cent increase over 1993-94 and to 11974.7 million nuts in 1993-94 from 1,1240.9 million nuts in 1992-93 registering a 6.53 per cent increase over 1992-93. The year 2005-06 also showed an increasing trend. The increase in production in these years was mainly due to favourable climatic conditions.

From the table, it is also observed, that the production declined substantially to 12,129 million nuts in 1999-00 from 12,535.9 million nuts in 1998-99 registering 3.25 per cent shortfall over 1998-99, due to pests and diseases. In the year 2002-03 also, the production declined sharply by 822 million nuts over the previous year of 2001-02, registering 6.34 per cent reduction, due to substantial reduction in the area of coconut cultivation as well as unfavourable climatic conditions.

It is also inferred from the Table, that the trend value for coconut production showed an increasing trend. The trend value increased from 8,498.903 million nuts in 1986-87 to 14,377.23 million nuts in 2005-06.

Productivity of Coconut in India

The average yield of coconut per hectare, the percentage of increase or decrease in the yield and the trend values are exhibited in Table 4.12.

It is inferred from Table 4.12 that the yield of coconut per hectare had registered a fluctuating trend during the period of study. The Table also reveals that the productivity of coconut per hectare ranged from 5,179 nuts to 7,608 nuts. The productivity per hectare increased from 5,401 nuts in 1987-88 to 5,992 nuts in 1988-89, registering 10.94 per cent increase in

Table 4.12. Trend in Coconut Productivity in India from 1986-87 to 2005-06

Year	Production (nuts per hectare)	Increase/ decrease	Percentage increase/ decrease	Trend value
1986-87	5179			6178.214
1987-88	5401	222	4.29	6230.944
1988-89	5992	591	10.94	6283.674
1989-90	6357	365	6.09	6336.405
1990-91	6407	50	0.79	6389.135
1991-92	6593	186	2.90	6441.865
1992-93	7310	717	10.88	6494.595
1993-94	7324	14	0.19	6547.325
1994-95	7760	436	5.95	6600.055
1995-96	7074	-686	-8.84	6652.785
1996-97	6908	-166	-2.35	6705.515
1997-98	6834	-74	-1.07	6758.245
1998-99	7145	311	4.55	6810.975
1999-00	6860	-285	-3.99	6863.705
2000-01	6847	-13	-0.19	6916.435
2001-02	6709	-138	-2.02	6969.165
2002-03	6345	-364	-5.43	7021.895
2003-04	6298	-47	-0.74	7074.626
2004-05	6632	334	5.30	7127.356
2005-06	7608	976	14.72	7180.086

Source: 1. Directorate of Economics and Statistics, Ministry of Agriculture, New Delhi.

2. Department of Economics and Statistics, Government of Kerala, Tiruvananthapuram.
3. Department of Statistics, Government of Tamil Nadu, Chennai.

the annual growth rate over 1987-88. The yield per hectare which stood at 7,760 nuts in 1994-95 decreased to 7,074 nuts in 1995-96, resulting in a negative annual growth rate of 8.84 per cent when compared to 1994-95.

The productivity levels of coconut output had also experienced a negative annual growth rate of 8.84 per cent, 2.35 per cent and 1.07 per cent, 3.99 per cent, 2.02 per cent and 5.43 per cent respectively during the years 1995-96, 1996-97, 1997-98, 1999-00, 2001-02 and 2002-03. The reasons attributed to the negative annual growth rate of productivity are unfavourable climatic conditions, severe attack of diseases and fluctuations in the price of coconut. It is also observed from the table, that the annual growth rate of coconut productivity increased by 10.94 per cent in 1988-89, 6.09 per cent in 1989-90, 5.95 per cent in 1994-95 and 14.72 per cent in 2005-06 when compared to the previous years because of conducive climatic conditions during these years. It is seen from the above Table that the trend value of productivity of coconut in India registered an increasing trend. It had increased from 6,178.214 nuts in 1986-87 to 7,180.086 nuts in 2005-06.

Compound Growth Rate and Magnitude of Variability

The Compound growth rate and magnitude of variability of area, production and productivity of coconut in India are presented in Table 4.13 *(See on next page)*.

Growth Rate

It could be observed from Table 4.13, that coconut production in India increased by 7.10 per cent per annum during the period under review. The area as well as productivity had also increased by 5.12 per cent and 1.98 per cent per annum respectively. Thus, it is observed that the increase in production was the result of increase in both area of cultivation and productivity.

Table 4.13. Trend Coefficient, Growth Rate and Magnitude of Variability of Coconut Cultivation in India from 1986-87 to 2005-06

Countries	Semi–log		R^2	CGR (Per cent/ Annum)	CV (Per cent)
	Constant	Regression Co-efficient			
Area	7.202 (0.024)	0.02167** (0.002)	0.865	5.12	13.10
Production	9.040 (0.326)	0.0297 NS (0.027)	0.062	7.10	19.10
Productivity	8.712 (0.042)	0.00856* (0.004)	0.246	1.98	9.83

Source: Computed Data

* Significant at five per cent level

** Significant at one per cent level

NS—Not Significant

Magnitude of Variability

It is also seen from Table 4.13, that coconut production in India experienced a considerable variation of 19.10 per cent during the period of study. The variation in productivity was 9.83 per cent, whereas it was 13.10 per cent in the case of area under cultivation of coconut.

Area under Coconut Cultivation in Tamil Nadu

The area under coconut cultivation, their relative changes over the previous years and the trend values are shown in Table 4.14 *(See on next page)*.

It is observed from Table 4.14, that area under coconut cultivation in Tamil Nadu which stood at 1,74,875 hectares in 1986-87 had increased to 3,70,515 hectares in 2005-06. Thus, the area under coconut cultivation has been increasing gradually during the period of study, except during 1998-99. The area had increased from 1,74,875 hectares in 1986-87 to 1,89,535 hectares in 1987-88, making an annual growth rate of 8.38 per cent when compared to 1986-87. The area under

Table 4.14. Trend in Area under Coconut Cultivation in Tamil Nadu from 1986-87 to 2005-06

Year	Area (hectare)	Increase\ decrease	Percentage increase\ decrease	Trend value
1986-87	174875			199726.1
1987-88	189535	14660	8.38	209160.6
1988-89	209234	19699	10.39	218595.1
1989-90	225862	16628	7.95	228029.6
1990-91	227171	1309	0.58	237464.1
1991-92	240300	13129	5.78	246898.6
1992-93	282109	41809	17.40	256333.1
1993-94	272823	-9286	-3.29	265767.6
1994-95	298588	25765	9.44	275202.1
1995-96	322549	23961	8.02	284636.6
1996-97	328020	5471	1.70	294071
1997-98	351841	23821	7.26	303505.5
1998-99	274877	-76964	-21.87	312940
1999-00	304028	29151	10.61	322374.5
2000-01	323485	19457	6.40	331809
2001-02	335632	12147	3.76	341243.5
2002-03	345866	10234	3.05	350678
2003-04	352710	6844	1.98	360112.5
2004-05	357056	4346	1.23	369547
2005-06	370515	13459	3.77	378981.5

Source: 1. Directorate of Economics and Statistics, Ministry of Agriculture, New Delhi.

2. Department of Economics and Statistics, Government of Kerala, Tiruvananthapuram.

3. Department of Statistics, Government of Tamil Nadu, Chennai.

coconut cultivation which stood at 2,09,234 hectares in 1988-89 had increased to 2,82,109 hectares in 1992-93, registering an annual growth rate of 17.40 per cent over the previous year.

The year 1999-00 showed an increasing percentage of 10.61 per cent with an increase of 29,151 hectares. The production of coconut during the year 1993-94 and 1998-99 had shown a decreasing trend with a decrease in area from 282109 hectares in 1992-93 to 27,282 hectares and from 3,51,841 hectares in 1997-98 to 2,74,877 hectares in 1998-99, registering decrease of 3.29 per cent and 21.87 per cent respectively. It is also inferred from the table that the trend value for area under coconut cultivation in Tamil Nadu increased from 1,99,726.1 hectares in 1986-87 to 3,78,981.5 hectares in 2005-06.

Coconut Production in Tamil Nadu

Production of coconut in Tamil Nadu, their percentage of increase or decrease over the previous years and the trend values are presented in Table 4.15.

It is observed from Table 4.15, that production of coconut in Tamil Nadu showed fluctuations from 1986-87 to 2005-06. The production had increased from 1,380.8 million nuts in 1986-87 to 1,578.3 million nuts in 1987-88 and to 1,920.5 million nuts in 1988-89, showing 14.30 per cent increase while comparing the previous year 1987-88. The production of coconut which stood at 2,560.5 million nuts in 2003-04 had increased to 4097 million nuts in 2004-05, registering 60 per cent increase in the annual growth rate when compared to 2003-04.

The years 1996-97, 1997-98 and 2001-02 also witnessed a substantial increase in production, with the annual growth rate of 19.98 per cent, 14.33 per cent and 3.18 per cent respectively when compared to the previous years, owning

Table 4.15. Trend in Coconut Production in Tamil Nadu from 1986-87 to 2005-06

Year	Production (million nuts)	Increase/ decrease	Percentage increase/ decrease	Trend value
1986-87	1380.8			2127.777
1987-88	1578.3	197.5	14.30	2231.756
1988-89	1920.5	342.2	21.68	2335.735
1989-90	2302.4	381.9	19.89	2439.713
1990-91	2498.8	196.4	8.53	2543.692
1991-92	2755.8	257	10.28	2647.671
1992-93	3364.6	608.8	22.09	2751.649
1993-94	3311.4	-53.2	-1.58	2855.628
1994-95	4345.7	1034.3	31.23	2959.607
1995-96	3257.6	-1088.1	-25.04	3063.586
1996-97	3810.6	553	19.98	3167.564
1997-98	4356.8	546.2	14.33	3271.543
1998-99	3335.6	-1021.5	-23.45	3375.522
1999-00	3222	-113.3	-3.40	3479.501
2000-01	3192	-30	-0.93	3583.479
2001-02	3293.6	101.6	3.18	3687.458
2002-03	2860.7	-432.9	-13.14	3791.437
2003-04	2560.5	-300.2	-10.49	3895.415
2004-05	4097	1536.5	60.01	3999.394
2005-06	4867.1	770.1	18.80	4103.373

Source: 1. Directorate of Economics and Statistics, Ministry of Agriculture, New Delhi.

2. Department of Economics and Statistics, Government of Kerala, Tiruvananthapuram.

3. Department of Statistics, Government of Tamil Nadu, Chennai.

to better climatic conditions. The year 1995-96 experienced a substantial decrease in annual growth rate by 25.04 per cent over the previous year. The erratic monsoon patterns and unfavourable climatic conditions were the major reasons for such drastic reduction in production during the year 1995-96. It is found from the table that the coconut production in Tamil Nadu had shown, generally, an increasing trend. The trend value increased from 2,127.777 million nuts in 1986-87 to 4,103.373 million nuts in 2005-06.

Productivity of Coconut in Tamil Nadu

Productivity of coconut during the period 1986-87 to 2005-06 the percentage of change over the previous years and trend values are presented in Table 4.16 *(See on next page)*.

It is observed from Table 4.16, that the yield of coconut per hectare in Tamil Nadu showed fluctuating trend during the period of study. The productivity of coconut per hectare ranged between 7,260 nuts per hectare and 16,117 nuts per hectare during 1986-87 to 2005-06. The Table reveals that productivity of coconut per hectare decreased from 10598 nuts in 1999-2000 to 9,868 nuts in 2000-01, indicating a negative annual growth rate of 6.89 per cent over the previous year 99-00, due to poor rainfall and unfavourable climatic conditions.

The year 2002-03 also experienced a decrease in the annual growth rate by 15.71 per cent, when compared to the previous year. The year 2004-05 witnessed a 58.04 per cent increase in the annual growth rate, over the previous year, due to favourable climatic conditions. It is also found from the table, that the trend value for productivity of coconut per hectare had increased from 14,849.97 in 1986-87 to 16,797.73 in 2005-06.

Table 4.16. Trend in Coconut Productivity in Tamil Nadu from 1986-87 To 2005-06

Year	Production (nuts per ha)	Increase\ decrease	Percentage increase\ decrease	Trend value
1986-87	7895			14849.97
1987-88	8327	432	5.47	14952.48
1988-89	9178	851	10.22	15055
1989-90	10193	1015	11.06	15157.51
1990-91	10999	806	7.91	15260.03
1991-92	11468	469	4.26	15362.54
1992-93	11926	458	3.99	15465.05
1993-94	12137	211	1.77	15567.57
1994-95	14554	2417	19.91	15670.08
1995-96	10100	-4454	-30.60	15772.59
1996-97	16117	106017	1049.67	15875.11
1997-98	12383	-103734	-89.34	15977.62
1998-99	12134	-249	-2.01	16080.13
1999-00	10598	-1536	-12.66	16182.65
2000-01	9868	-730	-6.89	16285.16
2001-02	9813	-55	-0.56	165387.67
2002-03	8271	-1542	-15.71	16490.19
2003-04	7260	-1011	-12.22	16592.7
2004-05	11474	4214	58.04	16695.22
2005-06	11782	308	2.68	16797.73

Source:1. Directorate of Economics and Statistics, Ministry of Agriculture, New Delhi.

2. Department of Economics and Statistics, Government of Kerala, Tiruvananthapuram.

3. Department of Statistics, Government of Tamil Nadu, Chennai.

Compound Growth Rate and Magnitude of Variability

The annual compound growth rates of area, production and productivity of coconut and their magnitude of variability in Tamil Nadu are furnished in Table 4.17.

Table 4.17. Trend Coefficient, Growth Rate and Magnitude of Variability of Coconut Cultivation in Tamil Nadu from 1986-87 to 2005-06

Countries	Semi-log		R^2	CGR (Per cent/ Annum)	CV (Per cent)
	Constant	Regression Co-efficient			
Area	12.186 (0.043)	0.0349** (0.004)	0.837	8.37	20.80
Production	7.590 (0.113)	0.03876** (0.009)	0.482	9.30	29.57
Productivity	9.327 (0.270)	0.00402 NS (0.023)	0.002	0.93	17.60

Source: Computed Data.
** Significant at one per cent level
NS—Not Significant

Growth Rate

It could be seen from Table 4.17 that during the study period between 1986-87 and 2005-06, there had been an increase in the production of coconut by 9.30 per cent per annum. There had also been an increase in the area of coconut cultivation by 8.37 per cent per annum and increase in productivity by 0.93 per cent per annum. Thus, it is inferred that the increase in area was the main factor which contributed to the increase in the growth rate in production.

Magnitude of Variability

It is also seen from the table that there was a variation of 29.57 per cent in the coconut production during the period of study. This variation was accompanied by wide variations in area 20.80 per cent and productivity 17.60 per cent.

Tamil Nadu's Share in All India Coconut Production

The All India production of coconut and Tamil Nadu's share and percentage of increase or decrease in its share are shown in Table 4.18.

Table 4.18. Production of Coconut in India and Tamil Nadu's Share from 1986-87 to 2005-06

Year	All India production (in million nuts)	Production in Tamil Nadu (in million nuts)	Share of Tamil Nadu (in per cent)
1986-87	6376.8	1380.8	21.65
1987-88	7269.9	1578.3	21.71
1988-89	8541.4	1920.5	22.48
1989-90	9358.8	2302.4	24.60
1990-91	9700.2	2498.8	25.76
1991-92	10079.6	2755.8	27.34
1992-93	11240.9	3364.6	29.93
1993-94	11974.7	3311.4	27.65
1994-95	13299.6	4345.7	32.68
1995-96	12952.3	3257.6	25.15
1996-97	13061	3810.6	29.18
1997-98	12717.3	4356.8	34.26
1998-99	12535.9	3335.3	26.61
1999-00	12129	3222	26.56
2000-01	12597.3	3192	25.34
2001-02	12963.2	3293.6	25.41
2002-03	12141.2	2860.7	23.56
2003-04	12178.2	2560.5	21.03
2004-05	12832.9	4097	31.93
2005-06	14811.1	4867.1	32.86
Average	11438.07	3115.58	26.78

Source: 1. Directorate of Economics and Statistics, Ministry of Agriculture, New Delhi.

2. Department of Economics and Statistics, Government of Kerala, Tiruvananthapuram.

3. Department of Statistics, Government of Tamil Nadu, Chennai.

It is inferred from Table 4.18, that the percentage share of Tamil Nadu in all India production ranged between 21.03 per cent and 34.26 per cent during the period of study. On an average, the volume of production of coconut in Tamil Nadu to that of India stood at 26.78 per cent. Tamil Nadu contributed a maximum of 34.26 per cent during the year 1997-98. The share of Tamil Nadu in all India coconut production, which stood at 21.65 per cent in 1986-87, increased to 21.71 per cent in 1987-88, 22.48 per cent in 1988-89, 24.60 per cent in 1989-90, 25.76 per cent in 1990-91, 27.34 per cent in 1991-92, 29.93 per cent in 1992-93, 27.65 per cent in 1993-94, 32.68 per cent in1994-95, 34.26 per cent in 1997-98, 31.93 per cent in 2004-05 and 32.86 per cent in 2005-06 respectively.

In the year 1993-94, there was a slight decrease in the share of Tamil Nadu, amounting to 27.65 per cent from 29.93 per cent in 1992-93. The years 1998-99, 1999-2000, 2000-01, 2002-03 and 2003-04 also experienced a negative annual growth, at the rates of 26.61 per cent, 25.34 per cent, 25.41per cent, 23.56 per cent and 21.03 per cent respectively over the corresponding previous years.

Area under Coconut Cultivation in Kanyakumari District

Kanyakumari is the second smallest district in Tamil Nadu, with an area of 1,672 sq. km. This district has a purely agricultural economy. Among commercial crops, rubber, coconut and cashew nut occupy the major parts of the area. Coconut alone is being raised in around 24,220 hectares. Area under coconut cultivation in the district has undergone dynamic increase from 17,284 hectares in 1986-1987 to 24,220 hectares in 2005-06.

Kanyakumari District also occupies a pre-dominant position in the area and production of coconut in Tamil Nadu. Coconut is cultivated, mostly, in all parts of the districts of Tamil Nadu. Kanyakumari District is next to Coimbatore District in coconut production, area under coconut cultivation and coconut productivity. The trend in coconut production, area under coconut cultivation and coconut productivity in Kanyakumari District are discussed here.

The area under coconut cultivation, their relative changes over the previous years and the trend values are shown in Table 4.19 *(See on next page)*.

It is observed from Table 4.19 that the area under coconut cultivation in Kanyakumari District which stood at 17,284 hectares in 1986-87 had increased to 24,220 hectares in 2005-06. Thus, the area under coconut cultivation had been increasing gradually during the period of study. The area had increased from 17284 hectares in 1986-87 to 17,342 hectares in 1987-98, making an annual growth rate of 0.34 per cent when compared to 1986-87. The area under coconut cultivation which stood at 17,492 hectares in 1988-89 had increased to 18,152 hectares in 1989-90, registering an annual growth rate of 3.77 per cent over the previous year.

The years since 1990-91 had shown an increasing percentage of 1.12 per cent, 0.77 per cent, 1.14 per cent, 2.49 per cent, 2.71 per cent, 5.22 per cent, and a maximum of 7.58 per cent increase in hectares during the respective years. It is a notable feature, that the production of coconut has not decreased during any year during the period of study. It is also inferred from the table that the trend value for area under coconut cultivation in Kanyakumari District had increased from 16,968.59 hectares in 1986-87 to 23,780.31 hectares in 2005-06.

Coconut Production in Kanyakumari District

Production of coconut in Kanyakumari District, the percentage increase or decrease over the previous years and the trend values are presented in Table 4.20 *(See on page 104)*.

It is observed from Table 4.20 that production of coconut in Kanyakumari District had been fluctuating from 1986-87 to 2005-06. The production had increased from 1209 lakh nuts in 1986-87 to 1512 lakh nuts in 1987-88, 1652 lakh nuts in

Table 4.19. Trend in Area under Coconut Cultivation in Kanyakumari District from 1986-87 to 2005-06

Year	Production (nuts per ha)	Increase/ decrease	Percentage increase/ decrease	Trend value
1986-87	17284			16968.59
1987-88	17342	58	0.34	17327.1
1988-89	17492	150	0.86	17685.61
1989-90	18152	660	3.77	18044.12
1990-91	18355	203	1.12	18402.63
1991-92	18496	141	0.77	18761.15
1992-93	18707	211	1.14	19119.66
1993-94	19173	466	2.49	19478.17
1994-95	19692	519	2.71	19836.68
1995-96	20719	1027	5.22	20195.19
1996-97	21100	381	1.84	20553.71
1997-98	21197	97	0.46	20912.22
1998-99	21514	317	1.50	21270.73
1999-00	21670	156	0.73	21629.24
2000-01	21946	276	1.27	21987.75
2001-02	22057	111	0.51	22346.27
2002-03	22187	130	0.59	22704.78
2003-04	22250	63	0.28	23063.29
2004-05	23936	1686	7.58	23421.8
2005-06	24220	284	1.19	23780.31

Source: 1. Directorate of Economics and Statistics, Ministry of Agriculture, New Delhi.

2. Department of Economics and Statistics, Government of Kerala, Tiruvananthapuram.

3. Department of Statistics, Government of Tamil Nadu, Chennai.

1988-89, 1824 lakh nuts in 1989-90, 1927 lakh nuts in 1990-91 and to a maximum of 3401 lakh nuts in 1999-2000. It had also increased to 3401 lakh nuts in 1999-2000 from 1927 lakh nuts

Table 4.20. Trend in Coconut Production in Kanyakumari District from 1986-87 to 2005-06

Year	Production (lakh nuts)	Increase/ decrease	Percentage increase/ decrease	Trend value
1986-87	1209			1786.4
1987-88	1512	303	25.06	1854.705
1988-89	1652	140	9.26	1923.011
1989-90	1824	172	10.41	1991.316
1990-91	1927	103	5.65	2059.621
1991-92	2038	111	5.76	2127.926
1992-93	2128	90	4.42	2196.232
1993-94	2348	220	10.34	2264.537
1994-95	2651	303	12.90	2332.842
1995-96	2899	248	9.35	2401.147
1996-97	3048	149	5.14	2469.453
1997-98	3190	142	4.66	2537.758
1998-99	3377	187	5.86	2606.063
1999-00	3401	24	0.7	2674.368
2000-01	3264	-137	-4.03	2742.674
2001-02	2702	-562	-17.22	2810.979
2002-03	2436	-266	-9.84	2879.284
2003-04	2288	-148	-6.08	2947.589
2004-05	2392	104	4.55	3015.895
2005-06	2420	28	1.17	3084.2

Source: 1. Directorate of Economics and Statistics, Ministry of Agriculture, New Delhi.

2. Department of Economics and Statistics, Government of Kerala, Tiruvananthapuram.

3. Department of Statistics, Government of Tamil Nadu, Chennai.

in1990-91, showing an increasing trend of 0.7 per cent. The production of coconut which stood at 2288 lakh nuts in 2003-04 had increased to 2392 lakh nuts in 2004-05, registering 4.55 per cent increase in the annual growth rate when compared to 2003-04.

The years 2000-2001, 2001-2002, 2002-2003 and 2003-2004 witnessed a substantial decrease in production, with annual negative growth rate of 4.03 per cent, 17.22 per cent, 9.84 per cent and 6.08 per cent respectively, when compared to the previous years owning to poor climatic conditions. The erratic monsoon patterns and unfavourable climatic conditions were the major reasons for such drastic reduction in production during the years. It is found from the table that the coconut production in Kanyakumari District had generally shown an increasing trend. The trend value had increased from 1786.40 lakh nuts in 1986-89 to 3084.20 lakh nuts in 2005-06.

Productivity of Coconut in Kanyakumari District

The productivity of coconut in Kanyakumari District, the percentage increase or decrease over the previous years and the trend values are presented in Table 4.21.

It is observed from Table 4.21, that productivity of coconut in Kanyakumari District had been fluctuating from 1986-87 to 2005-06. The production had increased from 6,995 nuts per hectare in 1986-87 to 8,719 nuts per hectare in 1987-88, 9,444 in 1988-89, 10,048 in 1989-90, 10,499 nuts per hectare in 1990-91 and increased to a maximum of 15,697 nuts per hectare in 1998-1999. Later, it had also increased to 12,250 nuts per hectare in 2001-02 from 12,246 nuts per hectare in 1993-94. The productivity of coconut which stood at 14,445 nuts per hectare in 1996-97 had increased to 15,049 nuts per hectare in 1997-1998, registering 4.18 per cent increase in the annual growth rate when compared to 1996-97.

The years 1999-2000, 2000-2001, 2001-2002, 2002-2003, 2003-2004, 2004-2005 and 2005-2006 witnessed a substantial decrease in productivity, with annual negative growth rate

Table 4.21. Trend in Coconut Productivity in Kanyakumari District from 1986-87 to 2005-06

Year	Productivity (nuts per ha)	Increase/ decrease	Percentage increase/ decrease	Trend value
1986-87	6995			10353.14
1987-88	8719	1724	24.65	10511
1988-89	9444	725	8.32	10668.85
1989-90	10048	604	6.40	10826.7
1990-91	10499	451	4.49	10984.56
1991-92	11019	520	4.95	11142.41
1992-93	11375	356	3.23	11300.25
1993-94	12246	871	7.66	11458.12
1994-95	13462	1216	9.93	11615.97
1995-96	13992	530	3.94	11773.82
1996-97	14445	453	3.24	11931.68
1997-98	15049	604	4.18	12089.53
1998-99	15697	648	4.31	12247.38
1999-00	15695	-2	-0.01	12405.24
2000-01	14873	-822	-5.24	12563.09
2001-02	12250	-2623	-17.64	12720.94
2002-03	10979	-1271	-10.38	12878.8
2003-04	10283	-696	-6.34	13036.65
2004-05	9993	-290	-2.82	13194.5
2005-06	9992	-1	-0.01	13352.36

Source:1. Directorate of Economics and Statistics, Ministry of Agriculture, New Delhi.

2. Department of Economics and Statistics, Government of Kerala, Tiruvananthapuram.

3. Department of Statistics, Government of Tamil Nadu, Chennai.

of 0.01 per cent, 5.24 per cent, 17.64 per cent 10.38 per cent, 6.34 per cent, 2.82 per cent and 0.01 per cent respectively when compared to the previous years, owing to poor climatic conditions. The erratic monsoon patterns and unfavourable climatic conditions were the major reasons for such drastic reduction in productivity during the years. It is found from the table that the coconut productivity in Kanyakumari District had shown generally an increasing trend. The trend value had increased from 10353.14 in 1986-87 to 13352.36 in 2005-06.

Production of Coconut in India and the Share of Kanyakumari District

The production of coconut in India and the share of Kanyakumari District are presented in Table 4.22 *(See on next page)*.

It is inferred from Table 4.22, that the percentage share of Kanyakumari District in the all India production of coconut, ranged between 1.63 per cent and 2.80 per cent during the period of study. On an average the percentage of the volume of production of coconut in Kanyakumari District to all India stood at 2.13. Kanyakumari District contributed the maximum of 2.80 per cent of the total world production during the year 1999-2000. The share of Kanyakumari District in all India coconut production which stood at 1.90 per cent in 1986-87, increased to 2.08 per cent in 1987-88, 1.93 per cent in 1988-89, 1.95 per cent in 1989-90, 1.99 per cent in 1990-91, 2.02 per cent in 1991-92, 1.96 per cent in 1993-94, 1.99 per cent in1994-95, 2.24 per cent in 1995-96, 2.69 per cent in 1998-99 and 2.80 per cent in 1999-2000.

In the year 1992-93, there was a slight decrease in the share of Kanyakumari District, 1.89 per cent from 2.02 per cent in 1991-92. The years 2000-01, 2001-02, 2002-03, 2003-04, 2004-05 and 2005-06 also experienced a negative annual growth rate of coconut production of 2.59 per cent, 2.08 per cent, 2.01per cent, 1.88 per cent 1.86 per cent, and 1.63 per cent respectively over the previous years.

Table 4.22. Production of Coconut in India and the Share of Kanyakumari District from 1986-87 to 2005-06

Year	All India Production (in million nuts)	Production in Tamil Nadu (in million nuts)	Production in Kanyakumari District. (in million nuts)	Share of Kanyakumari District (per cent)	
				India	Tamil Nadu
1986-87	6376.8	1380.8	120.9	1.90	8.76
1987-88	7269.9	1578.3	151.2	2.08	9.58
1988-89	8541.4	1920.5	165.2	1.93	8.60
1989-90	9358.8	2302.4	182.4	1.95	7.92
1990-91	9700.2	2498.8	19237	1.99	7.71
1991-92	10079.6	2755.8	203.8	2.02	7.40
1992-93	11240.9	3364.6	212.8	1.89	6.32
1993-94	11974.7	3311.4	234.8	1.96	7.09
1994-95	13299.6	4345.7	265.1	1.99	6.10
1995-96	12952.3	3257.6	289.9	2.24	8.90
1996-97	13061	3810.6	304.8	2.33	8.00
1997-98	12717.3	4356.8	319	2.51	7.32
1998-99	12535.9	3335.3	337.7	2.69	10.13
1999-00	12129	3222	340.1	2.80	10.56
2000-01	12597.3	3192	326.4	2.59	10.23
2001-02	12963.2	3293.6	270.2	2.08	8.20
2002-03	12141.2	2860.5	243.6	2.01	8.52
2003-04	12178.2	4097	228.8	1.88	8.94
2004-05	12832.9	4867.1	239.2	1.86	5.84
2005-06	14811.1	3115.6	242	1.63	4.97
Average	11438.1	3115.6	243.5	2.13	8.05

Source: 1. Directorate of Economics and Statistics, Ministry of Agriculture, New Delhi.

2. Department of Economics and Statistics, Government of Kerala, Tiruvananthapuram.
3. Department of Statistics, Government of Tamil Nadu, Chennai.

It is also evident from Table 4.22, that the percentage share of Kanyakumari District in the Tamil Nadu coconut production ranged between 4.97 per cent and 10.56 per cent during the period of study. On an average, the volume of production of coconut in Kanyakumari District to that of Tamil Nadu stood at 8.05 per cent. Kanyakumari District contributed a maximum of 10.56 per cent of the state's production during the year 1999-2000. The share of Kanyakumari District in Tamil Nadu coconut production, which stood at 8.76 per cent in 1986-87, increased to 9.58 per cent in 1987-88, 8.60 per cent in 1988-89, 8.90 per cent in 1995-96, 10.13 per cent in 1998-99, 10.56 per cent in 1999-00, and 8.94 per cent in 2003-2004 respectively.

In the year 1988-89 there was a slight decrease in the share of Kanyakumari District in the state production, amounting to 8.60 per cent from 9.58 per cent in 1987-88. The years 1989-90, 1990-91, 1991-92, 1992-93, 1994-95, 1997-98, 2001-02, 2004-05 and 2005-06 also experienced negative annual growth rates of 7.92 per cent, 7.71 per cent, 7.40 per cent, 6.32 per cent 6.10 per cent, 8.00 per cent, 7.32 per cent, 8.20 per cent 5.84 and 4.97 per cent respectively over the previous years.

The average all India production of coconut is 11438.1, followed by 3115.6 in Tamil Nadu and 243.5 in Kanyakumari District.

Area under Coconut Cultivation in Different Taluks of Kanyakumari District

An analysis of the taluk-wise area in Kanyakumari District under coconut cultivation, the production of coconut and the productivity of coconut and their analysis namely trend, compound growth rate, co-efficient of correlation and co-efficient of variation have also been made and explained in this portion. Taluk-wise area under coconut cultivation in Kanyakumari District from 1986-87 to 2005-06 is presented in Table 4.23.

Table 4.23. Taluk-wise Area (In Ha) under Coconut Cultivation in Kanyakumari District from 1986-87 to 2005-06

Year	Agasthee-swaram	Kalkulam	Vilavancode	Thovalai	Total
1986-87	5703	6477	4099	1005	17284
1987-88	5732	6535	4073	1002	17342
1988-89	5793	6520	4130	1049	17492
1989-90	5801	6690	4588	1073	18152
1990-91	5866	6965	4423	1101	18355
1991-92	5870	7003	4512	1111	18496
1992-93	5906	7108	4581	1112	18707
1993-94	6145	7268	4605	1155	19173
1994-95	6296	7486	4697	1213	19692
1995-96	6716	8048	4709	1246	20719
1996-97	6781	8209	4767	1343	21100
1997-98	6917	8168	4767	1343	21195
1998-99	6935	8475	4766	1338	21514
1999-00	7071	8537	4778	1284	21670
2000-01	7371	8923	4360	1289	21943
2001-02	7460	8924	4360	1313	22057
2002-03	7485	8963	4401	1338	22187
2003-04	7493	8992	4415	1350	22250
2004-05	7874	9367	4959	1746	23946
2005-06	8048	9383	5063	1726	24220
Average	6663.15	7902.05	4552.65	1256.85	20374.7
Per cent	32.70	38.78	22.34	6.17	100
Rank	2	1	3	4	

Source: 1. Directorate of Economics and Statistics, Ministry of Agriculture, New Delhi.

2. Department of Economics and Statistics, Government of Kerala, Tiruvananthapuram.

3. Department of Statistics, Government of Tamil Nadu, Chennai.

It is evident from Table 4.23, that among the taluks of the Kanyakumari District, Kalkulam taluk ranked first with an average area of 7,902.05 hectares out of the total average area of 20,374.7 contributing 38.78 per cent to the total area of coconut cultivation in the district. The trend in area of coconut cultivation in the Kalkulam taluk had increased from 6477 hectares in 1986-87 to 9,383 hectares in 2005-06. Agasteeswaram taluk ranked second, with an average area of 6,663.15 hectares out of the total average area of 20,374.7 contributing 32.70 per cent to the total area of coconut cultivation. The trend in area of coconut cultivation in the taluk, had shown an increasing trend from 5,703 hectares in 1986-87 to 8048 hectares in 2005-06.

Similarly, the Vilavancode taluk ranked third with an average area of 4,552.65 hectares out of the total average area of 2,0374.7, constituting 22.34 per cent of the total area of coconut cultivation. The trend in area of coconut cultivation in the taluk has increased from 4,099 hectares in 1986-87 to 5,063 hectares in 2005-06 with some increase and decrease here and there. The Thovalai taluk ranked the last, with an average area of 1,256.85 hectares out of the total average area of 2,0374.7, contributing 6.17 per cent to the total area of coconut cultivation. The trend in area of coconut cultivation in the taluk has increased continuously from 1,005 hectares in 1986-87 to 1,726 hectares in 2005-06.

Production of Coconut in Different Taluks of Kanyakumari District

Data relating to taluk-wise production of coconut in Kanyakumari District from 1986-87 to 2005-06 is presented in Table 4.24.

As seen from Table 4.24, the production of coconut had varied in the different taluks of Kanyakumari District. Among the various taluks, Kalkulam taluk ranked first with an annual average production of 949.9 lakh nuts out of the overall average production of 2,435.7 lakh nuts, contributing

Table 4.24. Taluk-wise Coconut Production (Lakh Nuts) in Kanyakumari District from 1986-87 to 2005-06

Year	Agasthee-swaram	Kalkulam	Vilavancode	Thovalai	Total
1986-87	399	453	287	70	1209
1987-88	501	571	356	84	1512
1988-89	547	616	390	99	1652
1989-90	588	679	457	109	1833
1990-91	616	731	464	116	1927
1991-92	647	772	497	122	2038
1992-93	672	809	521	126	2128
1993-94	753	890	564	141	2348
1994-95	848	1008	632	163	2651
1995-96	940	1126	659	174	2899
1996-97	993	1178	684	193	3048
1997-98	1041	1229	718	202	3190
1998-99	1092	1335	751	199	3377
1999-00	1114	1345	752	190	3401
2000-01	1096	1327	649	192	3264
2001-02	913	1093	534	161	2701
2002-03	786	1020	601	129	2536
2003-04	761	942	464	121	2288
2004-05	787	936	495	174	2392
2005-06	804	938	506	172	2420
Annual Average	794.9	949.9	544.05	146.85	2435.7
Per cent	32.64	39.00	22.34	6.03	100.00
Rank	2	1	3	4	

Source: 1. Directorate of Economics and Statistics, Ministry of Agriculture, New Delhi.

2. Department of Economics and Statistics, Government of Kerala, Tiruvananthapuram.

3. Department of Statistics, Government of Tamil Nadu, Chennai.

39 per cent to the total production of coconut. The trend in production of coconut in the taluk has increased from 453 lakh nuts in 1986-87 to 1,345 lakh nuts in 1999-2000 and has reduced to 938 lakh nuts in 2005-06. Agasteeswaram taluk ranked second with an annual average production of 794.9 lakh nuts out of the overall annual average coconut production of 2,435.7 lakh nuts contributing 32.64 per cent to the overall average production of coconut. The trend in production of coconut in the taluk has shown an increasing trend from 399 lakh nuts in 1986-87 to 804 lakh nuts in 2005-06.

Similarly the Vilavancode taluk ranked third, with an average production of coconut of 544.05 lakh nuts, out of the overall average production of 2,435.7 lakh nuts, contributing 22.34 per cent to the overall average production of coconut. The trend in production of coconut in the taluk has increased from 287 lakh nuts in 1986-87 to 506 lakh nuts in 2005-06, with some increase and decrease here and there. Thovalai taluk ranked the last with an annual average production of coconut of 146.85 lakh nuts out of the annual average production of 2,435.7 lakh nuts contributing 6.03 per cent to the overall average production of coconut. The trend in production of coconut in the taluk, has increased with some ups and downs from 70 lakh nuts in 1986-87 to 172 lakh nuts in 2005-06.

Productivity of Coconut in Different Taluks of Kanyakumari District

Data relating to the taluk-wise productivity of coconut in nuts per hectare in Kanyakumari District from 1986-87 to 2005-06 are presented in Table 4.25.

Table 4.25 reveals that, the productivity of coconut varies in the different taluks of Kanyakumari District. Among the various taluks, Kalkulam taluk ranked first with an average productivity of coconut of 11,890.1 nuts per hectare out of the over all average productivity of 47,190.45 nuts per hectare, contributing 25.20 per cent to the overall average productivity of coconut. The trend in productivity of coconut in the taluk

Table 4.25. Taluk-wise Coconut Productivity (*Nuts per Hectare*) in Kanyakumari District from 1986-87 to 2005-06

Year	Agasthee-swaram	Kalkulam	Vilavancode	Thovalai	Total
1986-87	6996	6994	7002	6965	27957
1987-88	8740	8738	8740	8383	34601
1988-89	9442	948	9443	9136	28969
1989-90	10136	10150	9960	10158	40404
1990-91	10501	10495	1049	10536	32581
1991-92	11022	11024	11015	10981	44042
1992-93	11378	11382	11373	11331	45464
1993-94	12254	12245	12248	12208	48955
1994-95	13469	13465	13455	13438	53827
1995-96	13996	13991	13994	13965	55946
1996-97	14644	14350	14349	14371	57714
1997-98	15050	15047	15056	15041	60194
1998-99	15746	15752	15757	14873	62128
1999-00	15754	15755	15760	14797	62066
2000-01	14869	14872	14855	14895	59491
2001-02	12239	12248	12248	12262	48997
2002-03	10501	11380	11384	9641	42906
2003-04	10156	10476	10150	8963	39745
2004-05	9995	9993	9982	9665	39635
2005-06	9990	9997	9994	9965	39946
Annual Average	11843.9	11890.1	11862.75	11593.7	47190.45
Per cent	25.10	25.20	25.14	24.57	100.00
Rank	3	1	2	4	

Source: 1. Directorate of Economics and Statistics, Ministry of Agriculture, New Delhi.

2. Department of Economics and Statistics, Government of Kerala, Tiruvananthapuram.

3. Department of Statistics, Government of Tamil Nadu, Chennai.

has increased from 6,994 nuts per hectare in 1986-87 to 15755 nuts per hectare in 1999-2000 and then had decreased from 14,872 nuts in 2001-02 to 9,997 nuts per hectare in 2005-06. Vilavancode taluk ranked second with an average productivity of 11862.75 nuts per hectare out of the over all average coconut productivity of 47,190.45 nuts per hectare contributing 25.14 per cent to the overall average productivity of coconut. The trend in productivity of coconut in the taluk had shown an increasing trend from 7,002 nuts per hectare in 1986-87 to 15,760 nuts per hectare in 1999-2000 but it decreased to 9,994 nuts per hectare in 2005-06.

Similarly, the Agasteeswaram taluk ranked third with an average productivity of 11,843.9 nuts per hectare, out of the overall average productivity of 47,190.45 nuts per hectare contributing 25.10 per cent to the overall average productivity of coconut. The trend in productivity of coconut in the taluk had increased from 6,996 nuts per hectare in 1986-87 to 15,754 nuts per hectare in 1999-2000 and it started decreasing and reached 9,990 nuts per hectare in 2005-06. Thovalai taluk ranked the last with an average productivity of 11,593.7 nuts per hectare out of the total productivity of 47,190.45 nuts per hectare, contributing 24.57 per cent to the total productivity of coconut. The trend in productivity of coconut in the taluk had increased with some variations during some years from 6,965 nuts per hectare in 1986-87 to 9965 nuts per hectare in 2005-06.

Trend Coefficient, Growth Rate and Magnitude of Variability

Taluk wise trend coefficient, growth rate and magnitude of variability of coconut in Kanyakumari District from 1986-87 to 2005-06 are depicted in Table 4.26.

Growth Rate (Agasteeswaram)

It could be seen from Table 4.26, that the area under coconut cultivation in Agasteeswarm Taluk, increased at the rate of

Table 4.26. Taluk-wise Trend Coefficient, Growth Rate and Magnitude of Variability of Coconut of Kanyakumari District from 1986-87 to 2005-06

Taluk	Semi-log		R^2	CGR (Per cent/ Annum)	CV (Per cent)
	Constant	Regression Co-efficient			
Area					
Agasthees-waram	8.593 (0.010)	0.01952 * (0.001)	0.967	4.6	11.80
Kalkulam	8.738 (0.010)	0.02182* (0.001)	0.975	5.15	12.93
Vilavancode	8.360 (0.023)	0.00592* (0.002)	0.337	1.37	5.99
Thovalai	6.874 (0.028)	0.02388* (0.002)	0.851	5.65	16.18
Kanyakumari District	9.731 (0.009)	0.01768* (0.001)	0.971	4.154	10.58
Production					
Agasthees-waram	6.288 (0.096)	0.3372* (0.008)	0.496	8.07	26.42
Kalkulam	6.426 (0.099)	0.0371* (0.008)	0.529	8.92	27.70
Vilavancode	6.044 (0.105)	0.02146* (0.009)	0.250	5.07	23.94
Thovalai	4.572 (0.104)	0.03586* (0.009)	0.489	8.61	27.49
Kanyakumari District	7.420 (0.098)	0.05255* (0.008)	0.466	7.78	26.06
Productivity					
Agasthees-waram	9.208 (0.097)	0.0142NS (0.008)	0.147	3.32	21.34
Kalkulam	9.201 (0.094)	0.01533* (0.008)	0.176	3.59	20.89
Vilavancode	9.200 (0.095)	0.01514* (0.008)	0.169	3.55	21.09
Thovalai	9.241 (0.101)	0.01159 NS (0.008)	0.095	2.70	21.54
Kanyakumari District	9.202 (0.095)	0.01487* (0.008)	0.164	3.48	21.13

Source: Compiled from Tables

*Significant at five per cent level

**Significant at one per cent level

NS—Not Significant

4.6 per cent per annum. There had also been an increase in the production of coconut at the rate of 8.07 per cent per annum and productivity at 3.32 per cent per annum. Thus, it is inferred from the table that the increase in area was the main factor which contributed to the increase in the growth rate of production.

Magnitude of Variability

It is seen from Table 4.26, that there was a considerable variation of 11.80 per cent in the area of coconut cultivation, 26.42 per cent in production and 21.34 per cent in productivity of coconut during the period of study.

Growth Rate (Kalkulam)

It could also be seen from Table 4.26, that the area under coconut cultivation in the Kalkulam Taluk increased at the rate of 5.15 per cent per annum. There had also been an increase in the production of coconut at the rate of 8.92 per cent per annum and increase in productivity at 3.59 per cent per annum. Thus, it is inferred from the table that the increase in area was the main factor which contributed to the increase in the growth rate of production.

Magnitude of Variability

It is also seen from Table 4.26, that there was a considerable variation of 12.93 per cent in the area of coconut cultivation, 27.70 per cent in the production of coconut and 20.89 per cent in the productivity of coconut during the period of study.

Growth Rate (Vilavancode)

It could be seen from Table 4.26, that the area under coconut cultivation in the Vilavancode Taluk, increased at the rate of 1.37 per cent per annum. There had also been an increase in the production of coconut at the rate of 5.07 per cent per annum and increase in productivity at 3.55 per cent per annum. Thus, it is inferred from the table, that the increase in area was the main factor which contributed to the increase in the growth rate of production.

Magnitude of Variability

It is seen from Table 4.26, that there was a considerable variation of 5.99 per cent in the area of coconut cultivation, 23.94 per cent in the production of coconut and 21.09 per cent in productivity of coconut during the period of study.

Growth Rate (Thovalai)

It could be seen from Table 4.26, that the area under coconut cultivation in Thovalai Taluk increased at the rate of 16.18 per cent per annum. There had also been an increase in the production of coconut at the rate of 8.61 per cent per annum and increase in productivity at 2.70 per cent per annum. Thus, it is inferred from the table, that the increase in area was the main factor which contributed to the increase in the growth rate of production.

Magnitude of Variability

It is seen from Table 4.26, that there was a considerable variation of 16.18 per cent in the area of coconut cultivation, 27.49 per cent in the production of coconut and 21.54 per cent in productivity of coconut during the period of study.

Growth Rate (Kanyakumari District)

It could also be seen from Table 4.26, that the area of coconut cultivation in the district, increased at the rate of 4.154 per cent per annum. There had also been an increase in the production of coconut by 7.78 per cent per annum and increase in productivity by 3.48 per cent per annum. Thus, it is inferred from the table that the increase in area was the main factor which contributed to the increase in the growth rate of production.

Magnitude of Variability

It is seen from Table 4.26, that there was a considerable variation of 10.58 per cent in the area of coconut cultivation, 26.06 per cent in the production of coconut and 21.13 per cent in productivity of coconut in the district during the period of study.

REFERENCES

1. Rajagopal V. *et. al.*, 'Coconut Industry-Improving Genetic Produce', *The Hindu, Survey of Indian Agriculture*, 2004, p. 67.
2. Ganesan K.P. 'Coconut Farming An Innovative Approach', *Kisan World*, Vol.28, No.8, August 2001, p. 53.
3. Narayan R.S. 'The Kalpagavriksha', *Kisan World*, Vol.21, No.7, July 1994, p. 59.

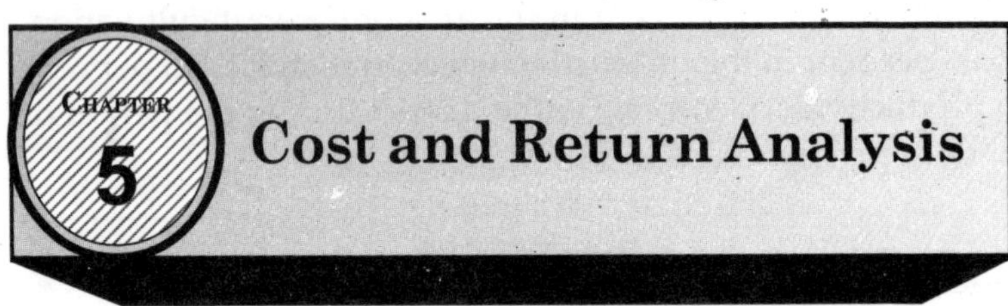

Introduction

An economic analysis of cost and returns, is an indicator of profitability in farming activity. However, a general descriptive analysis of costs and returns, is no substitute for a vigorous production function analysis which serves well as an indicator of the efficiency of factors' proportion in production. Nevertheless, a study of costs and returns, throws useful light on aspects which need careful scrutiny in a vigorous analysis. With this in view, an attempt was made to analyse cost and returns of coconut in the study region of Kanyakumari District.

The Establishment Cost of Coconut Cultivation

The average establishment cost of coconut cultivation for different farm groups, per acre, was worked out and the results are presented in Table 5.1.

It could be observed from Table 5.1 that the average total establishment cost of coconut cultivation for the first five years worked out to ₹ 127151.82 per acre in the case of marginal farmers, ₹ 127358.61 in the case of small farmers and ₹ 124338.38 in the case of large farmers. The net establishment cost, calculated by deducting the miscellaneous receipts from the total establishment cost, worked out to ₹ 11967.01 per acre in the case of marginal farmers, ₹ 116348.66 in the case of small farmers and ₹ 108475.78 in the case of large farmers.

Table 5.1. Establishment Cost of Production of Coconut

Sl. No.	Particulars	Marginal farmers		Small farmers		Large farmers	
		₹/Acre	%	₹/Acre	%	₹/Acre	%
I.	**A. Variable Cost**						
1.	Seedlings	1003.84	0.79	926.50	0.73	712.50	0.57
2	Labour	34400.00	27.05	32160.20	25.52	29898.25	24.05
3	Manure	14418.43	11.34	12615.70	9.91	10129.29	8.15
4	Fertilizer	2660.32	2.09	2510.64	1.97	2267.98	1.82
5	Pesticide	750.15	0.59	715.78	0.56	690.60	0.56
6	Interest on Working Capital	9315.73	7.33	8562.54	6.72	7647.26	6.15
7	Total Variable Cost	62548.47	49.19	57491.36	45.14	51345.88	41.30
II.	**B. Fixed Cost**						
8	Land Revenue Tax	750.00	0.59	750.00	0.59	750.00	0.60
9	Rental Value of Land	45000.00	35.39	45000.00	35.33	45000.00	36.19
10	Other Fixed Cost	18853.35	14.83	24117.25	18.94	27242.50	21.91
11	Total Fixed Cost	64603.35	50.81	69867.25	54.86	72992.50	58.70
12	Total Establishment Cost	127151.82	100.00	127358.61	100.00	124338.38	100.00
13	Less Misc. Receipts	7475.81		11009.95		15762.6	
14	Net Establishment cost	11967.01		116348.66		108475.78	
15	Annual Share of Net Establishment Cost	1595.68		1551.32		1447.68	

Source: Primary Data.

The annual share of net establishment cost, in the case of marginal farmers was ₹ 1595.68, where as it was ₹ 1551.32 in the case of small farmers and ₹ 1447.68 in the case of large farmers. While comparing the net establishment cost and the annual share of net establishment cost, it was found that the marginal farmers ranked first followed by the small and large farmers.

The total variable cost worked out to ₹ 62548.47, ₹ 57491.36 and ₹ 51345.88 respectively for marginal, small and large farmers. In other words, the total variable cost accounted for 49.19 per cent in the case of marginal farmers, 45.14 percent in the case of small farmers and 41.30 per cent in the case of large farmers. The contribution of fixed cost to the total establishment cost was ₹ 64603.35 (50.81%) for marginal farmers, ₹ 69867.25 (54.86%) for small farmers and ₹ 72992.50 (58.70%) for large farmers.

In the case of marginal farmers, of the total variable costs, human labour accounted for the maximum share of ₹ 34400 (27.05%) followed by cost of manure that accounted for ₹ 14418.43 (11.34%). The interest on working capital, borrowed for the purpose of cultivation, was estimated to be ₹ 9315.73 (7.33%) followed by cost of fertilizers amounting to ₹ 2660.32 (2.09%) and seedlings amounted to ₹ 1003.84 (0.79%). Besides these factors, the cost of pesticides accounted for about ₹ 750.15, which constituting 0.59 per cent of the total variable costs.

In the case of small farmers, of the total variable costs, human labour accounted for the maximum share of ₹ 32160.20 (25.25%) followed by cost of manure amounting to ₹ 12615.70 (9.91%). The interest on working capital, borrowed for the purpose of cultivation was estimated to be ₹ 8562.54 (6.72%) followed by cost of fertilizer which amounted to ₹ 2510.64 (1.97%) and seedlings amounting to ₹ 926.50 (0.73%). Besides these factors, the cost of pesticides accounted for about ₹ 715.78 which was 0.56 per cent of the total variable costs.

In the case of large farmers, of the total variable costs, human labour accounted for the maximum share of ₹ 29898.25 (24.05%) followed by cost of manure ₹ 10129.29 (8.15%). The interest on working capital borrowed for the purpose of cultivation was estimated to be ₹ 7647.26 (6.15%) followed by cost of fertilizers amounting to ₹ 2267.98 (1.82%) and seedlings amounting to ₹ 712.50 (57%). Besides these factors the cost of pesticides accounted for about ₹ 690.60 which constituted 0.56 per cent of the total variable costs.

On the whole, it was found that, human labour accounted for the maximum share of variable costs in the case of all the three categories of farmers.

The total fixed cost worked out to ₹ 64603.35, ₹ 69867.25 and ₹ 72992.50 respectively for marginal farmers, small and the large farmers. In other words, the total fixed cost accounted for 50.81 per cent in the case of marginal farmers, 54.86 per cent in the case of small farmers and 58.70 per cent in case of the large farmers. The contribution of fixed cost to the net establishment cost was ₹ 11967.01 for marginal farmers, ₹ 116348.66 for small farmers and ₹ 108575.78 for large farmers.

In the case of marginal farmers, of the total fixed costs, rental value of land accounted for the maximum share of ₹ 45000 (35.39%) followed by other fixed costs for ₹ 18853.35 (14.83%). Besides these factors, land revenue tax accounted for about ₹ 750 constituting 0.59 per cent of the total fixed costs. In the case of small farmers, of the total fixed costs, rental value of land accounted for the maximum share of ₹ 45000 (35.33%) followed by other fixed costs for ₹ 24117.25 (18.94%). Besides these factors land revenue tax accounted for about ₹ 750 constituting 0.59 per cent of the total fixed costs. In the case of large farmers, of the total fixed costs, rental value of land accounted for the maximum share of ₹ 45000 (36.19%) followed by other fixed costs for ₹ 27242.50 (21.91%). Besides these factors, land revenue tax accounted for about ₹ 750 constituting 0.60 per cent of the total fixed costs.

Cost of Coconut Cultivation

The average cost of coconut cultivation for different farm groups per acre was worked out and the results are presented in Table 5.2.

Table 5.2. Cost of Production of Coconut

Sl. No.	Particulars	Marginal farmers		Small farmers		Large farmers	
		₹/Acre	%	₹/Acre	%	₹/Acre	%
I.	**A. Variable Cost**						
1.	Labour cost	11814.10	36.65	10478.13	33.57	8871.64	29.14
2.	Cost of manure	3649.20	11.32	3010.61	9.65	3338.79	10.97
3.	Fertilizer cost	1298.50	4.03	1147.25	3.68	1199.66	3.94
4.	Cost of pesticide	355.00	1.10	520.98	1.67	500.07	1.64
5.	Interest on working Capital	599.09	1.86	530.49	1.70	486.86	1.60
6.	Total operation and maintenance cost	17715.89	54.96	15687.46	50.26	14397.02	47.29
II.	**B. Fixed Cost**						
7.	Land revenue tax	150.00	0.47	150.00	0.48	150.00	0.49
8.	Rental value of land	9000.00	27.92	9000.00	28.83	9000.00	29.56
9.	Other fixed cost	3770.67	11.70	4823.45	15.45	5448.50	17.90
10.	Annual share of net establishment cost	1595.68	4.95	1551.32	4.97	1447.68	4.76
11.	Total fixed cost	14516.35	45.04	15524.77	49.74	16046.18	52.71
12.	Total cost of production	32232.24	100.00	31212.23	100.00	30443.20	100.00

Source: Primary Data.

It could be observed from Table 5.2, that the average total cost of coconut production worked out to ₹ 32232.24 per acre in the case of marginal farmers, ₹ 31212.23 in the case of small farmers and ₹ 30443.20 in the case of large farmers. In other words, the total cost of coconut production was maximum in the case of marginal farmers, followed by small farmers and large farmers.

The total operational and maintenance costs worked out to ₹ 17715.89, ₹ 15687.46 and ₹ 14397.02 respectively for marginal, small and large farmers. In other words, the total operational and maintenance cost accounted for 54.96 per cent in the case of marginal farmers, 50.26 per cent in the case of small farmers and 47.29 per cent in the case of large farmers. The contribution of fixed cost to the total operational and maintenance cost was ₹ 14516.35 (45.04%) for marginal farmers, ₹ 15524.77 (49.74%) for small farmers and ₹ 16046.18 (52. 71%) for large farmers.

In the case of marginal farmers, of the total operational and maintenance cost, human labour cost accounted for the maximum share of ₹ 11814.10 (36.65%) followed by cost of manure for ₹ 3649.20 (11.32%). The cost of fertilizer was found to be ₹ 1298.50 (4.03%) and the interest on working capital borrowed for the purpose of cultivation was estimated to be ₹ 599.09 (1.86%). Besides these factors, the cost of pesticides accounted for about ₹ 355.00 which was 1.10 per cent of the total operational and maintenance costs.

In the case of small farmers, among the total operational and maintenance costs, human labour cost accounted for the maximum share of Rs.10478.13 (33.57%) followed by cost of manure for Rs.3010.61 (9.65%). The cost of fertilizer was found to be Rs.1147.25 (3.68%) and the interest on working capital borrowed for the purpose of cultivation was estimated to be Rs.530.49 (1.70%). Besides these factors, the cost of pesticides, accounted for about Rs.520.98 which constituted 1.67 per cent of the total operational and maintenance costs.

In the case of large farmers, of the total operational and maintenance costs, human labour cost accounted for the maximum share of ₹ 8871.64 (29.14%) followed by cost of manure for ₹ 3338.79 (10.97%). The cost of fertilizer was found to be ₹ 1199.66 (3.94%) and the cost of pesticides used during cultivation was estimated to be ₹ 500.07 (1.64%). Besides these factors, the interest on working capital, borrowed for the purpose of cultivation, accounted for about ₹ 486.86 which constituted 1.60 per cent of the total operational and maintenance costs.

To sum up, human labour accounted for the maximum share of operational and maintenance cost in all the three categories of farmers.

The total fixed costs, per acre, worked out to ₹ 14516.35, ₹ 15524.77 and ₹ 16046.18 respectively for marginal, small and the large farmers. In other words, the total fixed cost accounted for 45.04 per cent in the case of marginal farmers, 49.74 per cent in the case of small farmers and 52.71 per cent in the case of the large farmers. The contribution of fixed cost to the total cost of production was ₹ 32232.24 for marginal farmers, ₹ 31212.23 for small farmers and ₹ 30443.20 for larger farmers.

In the case of marginal farmers, of the total fixed costs, rental value of land accounted for the maximum share of ₹ 9000.00 (27.92%) followed by other fixed costs of ₹ 3770.67 (11.70%) and the annual share of net establishment cost accounted for Rs.1595.68(4.95). Besides these factors, land revenue tax accounted for about ₹ 150.00 which contributed 0.47 per cent of the total fixed costs. In the case of small farmers, of the total fixed costs, rental value of land accounted for the maximum share of ₹ 9000 (28.83%) followed by other fixed costs of ₹ 4823.45 (15.45%) and the annual share of net establishment cost accounted for ₹ 1551.32 (4.97%). Besides these factors, land revenue tax accounted for about ₹ 150 which contributed 0.48 per cent of the total fixed costs. In the case of large farmers, of the total fixed costs, rental value of land accounted for the maximum share of ₹ 9000 (29.56%) followed by other fixed costs of ₹ 5448.50 (17.90%) and the annual share of net establishment cost accounted for Rs.1447.68 (4.7%). Besides these factors, land revenue tax accounted for about ₹ 150 which contributed 0.49 per cent of the total fixed costs.

Productivity and Unit Cost of Production of Coconut

The average annual productivity and cost of production of coconut were worked out and the results are presented in Table 5.3.

Table 5.3. Average Annual Productivity and Unit Cost of Production

Sl.No.	Particulars	Marginal farmers	Small farmers	Large farmers
1	Trees (nos/acre)	91	85	75
2	Yield (nuts/acre)	6972	7125	7724
3	Yield per tree (nuts per annum)	77	84	103
4	Total Cost of cultivation (₹/acre)	32232.24	31212.23	30443.2
5	Cost of Production (₹/nut)	4.62	4.38	3.94

Source: Primary Data

It is evident from Table 5.3, that the total number of trees in an acre ranged from 75 trees in the case of large farmers to 91 trees in the case of marginal farmers. With regard to yield, number of nuts from one acre of coconut plantation, ranged from 7724 nuts per acre in the case of large farmers, to 6972 nuts per acre in the case of marginal farmers. The yield of coconut per tree, in terms of number of nuts per annum was the maximum in the case of large farmers with 103 nuts, followed by 84 nuts in the case of small farmers and 77 for marginal farmers.

The results of the analysis also indicated that the total cost of cultivation of coconut ranged from ₹ 32232.24 per acre in the case of marginal farmers to ₹ 30443.2 in the case of large farmers. The cost of production per nut, was ₹ 4.62 for marginal farmers, 4.38 for small farmers and ₹ 3.94 for large farmers.

Scientific method of cultivation, adopted by large farmers must have been the main reason for increasing output and reducing the cost of production.

Income Measures Over Different Cost Concepts

The various measures of return (income) over different cost concepts were measured and the details are presented in Table 5.4.

Table 5.4. Statement of Income in Coconut Cultivation

(₹/Acre/annum)

Sl. No.	Particulars	Marginal farmers	Small farmers	Large farmers
1.	Gross sales	39740.40	40897.50	44413.00
2.	Less—Marketing cost	847.35	802.69	763.29
3.	Gross returns	38893.05	40094.81	43649.71
4.	Less—Variable cost	17715.89	15687.46	14397.02
5.	Contribution	21177.16	24407.35	29252.69
6.	Less—Fixed cost	14516.35	15524.77	16046.18
7.	Net Profit	6660.81	8882.58	13206.51
8.	Net profit ratio	17.13	22.15	30.26
9.	Gross selling price	5.70	5.74	5.75
10.	Net Selling price	5.58	5.63	5.65

Source: Primary Data

It could be observed from Table 5.4, that the gross sales proceeds of coconut ranged from ₹ 44413 in the case of large farmers to ₹ 39740.40 in the case of marginal farmers with the highest gross return of ₹ 43649.71 for large farmers, followed by ₹ 40094.81 for small farmers and ₹ 38893.05 for marginal farmers in the study area. Both the marketing cost and variable cost were the highest i.e ₹ 847.35 and ₹ 17715.89 respectively for marginal farmers and ₹ 802.69 and ₹ 15687.46 respectively for small farmers.

The amount of contribution was estimated to be the maximum of ₹ 29252.69, ₹ 24407.35 and ₹ 21177.16 respectively in the case of large farmers, small farmers and marginal farmers. Similarly, the amount of fixed cost of production of coconut also ranged from ₹ 16046.18 in the case of large farmers and ₹ 14516.35 in the case of the marginal farmers. But the amount of ₹ 15524.77 was contributed as fixed cost for the small farmers.

The net profit ranged between ₹ 13206.51, the highest among large farmers, and the lowest of ₹ 6660.81 among marginal farmers. The net profit ratio was the highest in the case of large farmers i.e 30.26 and the lowest of 17.13, in the case of marginal farmers and 22.15 in the case of the small farmers. The gross selling price and the net selling price were calculated as 5.70, 5.74, 5.75 and 5.58, 5.63 and 5.65 respectively in the case of marginal farmers, small farmers and large farmers.

Functional Analysis

Production Function Analysis

The costs and return analysis showed that cultivation of coconut was profitable. The question whether there was any scope to increase the net returns per acre, could be answered by analyzing the resource-use-efficiency.

Among the different types of production functions, Cobb-Douglas Type Production Function (log-linear) was chosen, as it has the following advantages:

1. It was convenient to find out the elasticity of production which indicates the percentage change in input.
2. The sum of production elasticities (bi) indicates the nature of returns to scale.

Functional Analysis

The relationship between yield of coconut and different inputs was studied using multiple regression analysis

The function log form is as follows:

$$\text{Log } Y = \log a + b_1 \log x_1 \quad + b_2 \log x_2 + \ldots\ldots + b_6 \log x_6 + eu$$

where

Y = Yield in nuts per acre

X_1 = Cost of seedlings

X_2 = Labour in man days, per acre

X_3 = Cost of manure in rupees, per acre

X_4 = Cost of fertilizer in rupees, per acre

X_5 = Cost of pesticides in rupees, per acre

X_6= Number of coconut trees.

U = Error term

In order to test the significance of the estimated parameters, t-test using the following formula was used:

$$t = \frac{b_i}{SE(b_1)}$$

where

bi = Parameters to be estimated

SE(bi) = Standard Error of *bi*

(i.e.) $\sum bi, i = 1, 2, 3, 4, 5$

if

$\sum b_i < 1$ decreasing returns to scale

$b_i = 1$ constant returns to scale

$b_i > 1$ increasing returns to scale

Estimated Production Function of Coconut for Marginal Farmers

The Cobb-Douglas Type Production Function was fitted for marginal farmers. The results are presented in Table 5.5.

Table 5.5. Estimated Production Function of Coconut for Marginal Farmers

Sl.No	Variables	Symbol	Regression co-efficient	Standard Error
1.	Yield in nuts, per acre	Y	-	-
2.	Constant	b0	3.173*	0.826
3.	Cost of Seedlings	X1	0.139^{NS}	0.091
4.	Labour in man-days, per acre	X2	0.389*	0.057
5.	Cost of manure in rupees, per acre	X3	0.147*	0.020
6.	Cost of fertilizer in rupees, per acre	X4	0.258*	0.037
7.	Cost of pesticides in rupees, per acre	X5	0.281^{NS}	0.193
8.	Number of coconut trees	X6	-0.0657*	0.0286
	Sum of elasticity co-efficients R^2 0.819 *F*-test 18.759*		1.1483	

Source: Computed Data

Note: 1. * Significant at five per cent level

2. NS.—Not Significant

Table 5.5 shows, that the value of co-efficient of multiple determination (R^2) was 0.819 indicating that 82 per cent of variation in the yield could be explained by the independent variables that are included in the function. The regression co-efficients are partial elasticities of production of coconut, with respect to the inputs concerned. The yield of coconut was significantly influenced by the level of the labour utilized. One per cent increase in the level of labour used, keeping all other factors constant, would increase the yield by 0.389 per cent, in its mean level. The coconut yield was also significantly influenced by the level of total cost of fertilizer and total cost of manure. The analysis indicates that every one per cent increase in the level of fertilizer applied, ceteris paribus, could increase the yield by 0.258 per cent from its mean level. While one per cent increase in the level of manures used, ceteris paribus, could increase the yield by 0.147 per cent from its mean level. The analysis also indicates that relationship between cost of seedling and yield was positive, but not significant statistically. Therefore, the cost of seedling had no significant influence on the yield. The relationship between total number of coconut trees and yield was negative and statistically significant. It implies that one per cent increase in the number of trees would decrease the yield by 0.0657 per cent from its mean level.

Estimated Production Function of Coconut for Small Farmers

The long-linear production function was estimated for small farmers and the results are presented in Table 5.6.

Table 5.6 shows that the value of co-efficient of multiple determinations (R^2) was 0.873 which indicated that 87 per cent of variation in the yield, could be explained by the independent variables, that are included in the function. The regression co-efficients are partial elasticities of production of coconut, with respect to the inputs concerned. The yield of coconut was significantly influenced by the level of the labour utilized. One per cent increase in the level of labour used, keeping all other factors constant, would increase the yield by 0.241 per cent in its mean level.

Table 5.6. Estimated Cobb-douglas Production function for Small Farmers

Sl.No	Variables	Symbol	Regression co-efficient	Standard Error
1	Yield in nuts, per acre	Y	-	-
2	Constant	b0	6.611	0.92
3	Cost of Seedlings	X1	0.392^{NS}	0.438
4	Labour in man-days, per acre	X2	0.241*	0.081
5	Cost of manure in rupees, per acre	X3	0.295*	0.111
6	Cost of fertilizer in rupees, per acre	X4	0.199*	0.065
7	Cost of pesticides in rupees, per acre	X5	0.573^{NS}	0.524
8	Number of coconut trees	X6	-0.0972*	0.041
	Sum of elasticity co-efficients		1.6028	
	R^2		0.873	
	F-test		14.201*	

Source: Computed Data

Note: 1. * Significant at five per cent level

2. NS—Not Significant.

The coconut yield was also significantly influenced by the level of cost of fertilizer and cost of manure. The analysis indicates that every one per cent increase in the level of fertilizer applied, ceteris paribus could increase the yield by 0.199 per cent from its mean level while one per cent increase in the level of manures used, ceteris paribus, could increase the yield by 0.295 per cent from its mean level. The analysis also indicates that the relationship between the cost of seedlings and yield was positive, but not significant statistically. Therefore, the cost of seedlings had no significant influence on the yield. The relationship between the total number of coconut trees and yield was negative and statistically significant. It implies that one percent increase, in the number of trees, would decrease the yield by 0.0972 per cent from its mean level.

Estimated Production Function of Coconut for Large Farmers

The long-linear production function was estimated for large farmers and the results are presented in Table 5.7.

Table 5.7 shows that the value of co-efficient of multiple determinations (R^2) was 0.846 which indicates that 85 per cent of variation in the yield could be explained by the independent variables, that are included in the function. The regression co-efficients are partial elasticities of production of coconut with respect to the inputs concerned. The yield of coconut was significantly influenced by the level of the labour utilized. One per cent increase in the level of labour used, keeping all other factors constant, would increase the yield by 0.89 per cent in its mean level.

The coconut yield was also significantly influenced by the level of cost of fertilizer and cost of manure. The analysis indicates that every one per cent increase in the level of fertilizer applied ceteris paribus, could increase the yield by 0.237 per cent from its mean level, while one per cent increase in the level of manures used ceteris paribus, could increase the yield by 0.143 per cent from its mean level. The analysis also indicates that the relationship between the cost of seedlings and yield was positive, but not significant statistically. Therefore, the cost of seedlings had no significant influence on the yield. The relationship between the total number of coconut trees and yield was positive but statistically not significant. Therefore, the total number of coconut trees had no significant influence on the yield.

Table 5.7. Estimated Cobb-douglas Production function for Large Farmers

Sl.No	Variables	Symbol	Regression co-efficient	Standard Error
1	Yield in nuts, per acre	Y	-	-
2	Constant	b_0	0.912	0.294
3	Cost of Seedlings	X1	0.331^{NS}	0.262
4	Labour in man-days, per acre	X2	0.89*	0.024
5	Cost of manure in rupees, per acre	X3	0.143*	0.033
6	Cost of fertilizer in rupees, per acre	X4	0.237*	0.079
7	Cost of pesticides in rupees, per acre	X5	0.731^{NS}	0.698
8	Number of coconut trees	X6	0.0606^{NS}	0.246
	Sum of elasticity co-efficients		1.4704	
	R^2		0.846	
	F-test		26.74*	

Source: Computed Data

Note: 1. * Significant at five per cent level

2. NS—Not Significant

Returns to Scale

The sum of elasticities of resources is an indicator of the returns to scale. The analysis of the returns to scale, for different groups, were worked out and the results are presented in Table 5.8 *(See on next page)*.

Table 5.8 shows, that the sum of the elasticities were 1.1483 in marginal farmers, 1.6028 in small farmers and 1.4704 in large farmers, in coconut cultivation in the study region. It has been found that, there is no farm which has less than unity of elasticity. On the other hand, the sum of elasticities was greater than unity in all categories. The results showed that there was increasing return to scale in all categories of farmers in the study region.

Table 5.8. Nature of Return to Scale

Category	Sum of Production Elasticities	Nature of returns to scale
Marginal farmers	1.1483	Increasing
Small farmers	1.6028	Increasing
Large farmers	1.4704	Increasing

Source: Computed Data

Resource Use Efficiency

The marginal value productivity of resources and the cost of those resources, would give an indication for the reallocation of resources to maximize returns. Optimization principle in resource allocation, suggests that the application of the resources should be increased or decreased, till marginal value product of a resource equates its marginal cost. In the present study, marginal value product was calculated by using the following formula:

$$MVP_j = bj = \frac{\overline{Y}}{\overline{\overline{X}}j}P,$$

where,

MVP = Marginal value product for inputs (Xj)

b = Estimated elasticity co-efficient of variable (Xj)

Y = Geometric mean of yield (kg)

X = Geometric mean value of variable (Xj)

P = Mean net selling price of coconut (₹/nut)

For j = 1, 2, 3, ... 5

After computing *MVP* of various inputs, it was divided by marginal input cost or factor cost, to arrive at the ratio of marginal value product to the input cost.

Resource Use Efficiency Among Marginal Farmers

The marginal value productivity of the resource use efficiency among marginal farmers, was worked out from the production function analysis and the results are presented in Table 5.9.

Table 5.9. Marginal Value Productivity of the Resource Use Efficiency (Marginal Farmers)

Sl. No.	Variable	Particulars	Geometric mean	Average physical product	Elasticity co-efficient	Marginal Physical product	Marginal value	Marginal input	Marginal value produc-tivity
1	Y	Yield (nuts/acre)	6659						
2	X2	Labour in Mandays/ acre	44	151.341	0.389	58.872	328.50	215	1.53
3	X3	Cost of manure in ₹/acre	3199.2	2.081	0.147	0.306	1.71	1	1.71
4	X4	Cost of fertilizer in ₹/acre	1002.39	6.643	0.258	1.714	9.56	1	9.56
5	X6	No. of coconut trees	82	81.207	-0.0657	-5.335	—	—	—

Source: Computed Data

The results indicate that the marginal physical products of labour, cost of manure and cost of fertilizers were 58.872, 0.306 and 1.714 respectively. The marginal value of inputs were also ₹ 328.50, ₹ 1.71 and ₹ 9.56 respectively. It is inferred from Table 5.9, that there was scope for increasing use of labour, fertilizers and manures, to increase the yield of coconut further in the case of marginal farmers, as the ratio of marginal value product to factor cost was more than unity.

It also revealed that every rupee, additionally spent on those variables, would increase the value of yield further by ₹ 1.53, ₹ 1.71 and ₹ 9.56 respectively.

Resource use Efficiency in Small Farmers

The resource use efficiency was worked out for the small farmers and the results are presented in Table 5.10.

Table 5.10. Marginal Value Productivity of the Resource use Efficiency (Small Farmers)

Sl. No.	Variable	Particulars	Geometric mean	Average physical product	Elasticity co-efficient	Marginal Physical product	Marginal value	Marginal input	Marginal value produc-tivity
1	Y	Yield (nuts/ acre)	6883	—	—	—	—	—	—
2	X2	Labour in Mandays/acre	40	172.075	0.241	41.470	233.48	215	1.09
3	X3	Cost of manure in Rs./acre	2799.23	2.459	0.295	0.725	4.08	1	4.08
4	X4	Cost of fertilizer in Rs./ acre	899.59	7.651	0.199	1.523	8.57	4	8.57
5	X6	No. of coconut trees	82	83.939	-0.972	-8.159	—	—	—

Source: Computed Data

The results indicate that the marginal physical products of labour, cost of manure and cost of fertilizers were 41,470, 0.725 and 1.523 respectively. The marginal value of inputs were also ₹ 233.48, ₹ 4.08 and ₹ 8.57 respectively. It is inferred from the Table 5.10 that there was scope for increasing use of labour, fertilizers and manures to increase the yield of coconut further in the case of small farmers as the ratio of marginal value product to factor cost was more than unity. It also revealed that every rupee additionally spent on those variables, would increase the value of yield further by ₹ 1.09, ₹ 4.08 and ₹ 8.57 respectively.

Resource Use Efficiency In Large Farmers

The resource use efficiency for large farmers was analysed and the results are presented in Table 5.11.

Table 5.11. Marginal Value Productivity of the Resource use Efficiency (Large Farmers)

Sl. No.	Variable	Particulars	Geometric mean	Average physical product	Elasticity co-efficient	Marginal Physical product	Marginal value	Marginal input	Marginal value produc-tivity
1	Y	Yield (nuts/acre)	7438	—	—	—	—	—	—
2	X2	Labour in Mandays/ acre	37	201.027	0.089	17.891	101.09	215	0.47
3	X3	Cost of manure in ₹/acre	2983.92	2.493	0.143	0.356	2.01	1	1.01
4	X4	Cost of fertilizer in ₹/ acre	910.85	8.166	0.237	1.935	10.93	1	10.93

Source: Computed data.

The results indicate, that the marginal physical products of labour, cost of manure and cost of fertilizers were 17.891, 0.356 and 1.935 respectively. The marginal value of inputs were also ₹ 101.09, ₹ 2.01 and ₹ 10.93 respectively. It is inferred from Table 5.11, that there was scope for increasing the use of labour, fertilizers and manures to increase the yield of coconut further, in the case of large farmers, as the ratio of marginal value product to factor cost was more than unity, except labour. It is also revealed that every rupee additionally spent on those variables, would increase the value of yield further by ₹ 0.47, Rs.1.01 and ₹ 10.93 respectively. In total, it can be concluded that there is scope for increasing the coconut yield by better utilization of these variables.

Capital Productivity Analysis

Coconut being a perennial, commercial and a food crop, the commercial production starts from the fourth year onwards. So, considerable investments need to be made over several years, before the crop starts to yield. Moreover, the benefits are realized as a stream, over a long period of time. Therefore, it is necessary to know the present value of the expected future income, to justify the investments made. A sound appraisal technique should be used, to measure the economic worth of the investments made in coconut farms.

The Analytical Framework

In the present study, the following capital budgeting techniques are used to measure the economic worth of the investments in coconut production.

To compute the pay-back period, net present value and internal rate of return for coconut cultivation, incremental cost, present value of cost and returns at 10 per cent discount factor were calculated.

Pay-back Period

It measures the number of years required, to recover the original cash outlay invested in the project. The maximum acceptable pay back period is fixed by taking into account the reciprocal of the cost of capital. This can be termed as the cut-off point. The cut off year at 10 per cent cost of capital is 10 years. Generally, a project having a pay-back period, more than the cut-off point, is not entertained. The Pay-back period of coconut cultivation is calculated and presented in Table 5.12.

Table 5.12. Pay-back Period of Coconut Cultivation

Sl. No.	Type of farmers	Pay-back Period (year)	Cut off period (year)	Accept or reject criterion
1.	Marginal	10.43	10	Acceptable
2.	Small	9.75	10	Acceptable
3.	Large	8.19	10	Acceptable

Source: Computed Data

It could be inferred from Table 5.12, that the pay-back period of coconut cultivation was 10.43 years in the case of marginal farmers 9.75 years in the case of small farmers and only 8.19 years in the case of large farmers. The pay-back period has been less than 10 years, in all the categories of farmers, except the marginal. As the pay-back period is less than the cut-off period, in the case of small and large farmers, it can be decided that coconut cultivation is viable. It is also viable in marginal farmers as the difference is very meagre.

Net Present Value

The Net Present Value is found, by subtracting the present value of cost from the present value of returns. A project, whose net present value, is greater or equal to zero, is considered as a worthy investment.

Net present value = Present value of returns – Present value of costs

Symbolically

$$NPV = \sum_{t=1}^{n} \frac{Bt - Ct}{(1+i)t},$$

where the symbols used are the same, as in the case of benefit-cost ratio.

It is the most valid technique of evaluating an investment project. It is generally consistent with the objective of maximizing wealth. The Net Present Value of coconut cultivation was computed and is presented in Table 5.13.

Table 5.13. Net Present Value of Coconut Cultivation

Sl. No.	Type of farmers	Net present value (in ₹ Per acre)	Nature of Net Present Value
1	Marginal	36329.94	Positive
2	Small	61511.31	Positive
3	Large	95988.79	Positive

Source: Computed Data

It is observed from Table 5.13, that the net present value was estimated to be ₹ 36329.94 at 10 per cent discount rate, in the case of marginal farmers, followed by ₹ 61511.31 in the case of small farmers and the highest of ₹ 95988.79 in the case of large farmers. Since the net present value is positive and large, it is inferred that the capacity to generate more wealth is large in coconut farms. Therefore, the investment in coconut cultivation is economically beneficial.

Internal Rate of Return

The Internal Rate of Return is the rate of discount, at which NPV is zero. If the IRR exceeds the cut off rate (opportunity cost of capital) the investment is economically viable. Symbolically,

$$\text{IRR} = \sum_{t=1}^{n} \frac{Bt - Ct}{(1+i)t} = 0$$

The Internal Rate of Return of Coconut Cultivation is the rate at which the sum of discounted cash inflows, equals the sum of discounted cash outflows. It is the maximum rate of interest, which an organization can afford, to pay on the capital invested in a project. The results of the Internal Rate of Return of coconut cultivation are presented in Table 5.14.

Table 5.14. Internal Rate of Return of Coconut Cultivation

Sl. No.	Type of farmers	Internal Rate of Return (%)	Opportunity cost of capital (%)	Accept or reject criterion
1	Marginal	14.88	10	Acceptable
2	Small	16.60	10	Acceptable
3	Large	18.96	10	Acceptable

Source: Computed Data

It is evident from Table 5.14, that the computed value of Internal Rate of Return of Coconut cultivation was 14.88 per cent for the marginal farmers, followed by 16.60 per cent for small farmers and 18.96 for large farmers. As compared to the opportunity cost of capital (cut off rate) which was taken as 10 per cent, the rate of return on investment, made in coconut cultivation is high. It indicates that there is economic viability of investment in coconut cultivation.

Introduction

In the present world, production of goods, has meaning only when they are marketed. Marketing consists of a number of heterogeneous functions, besides selling, performed by different intermediaries in different periods of time, as the products are transferred from the producers to the ultimate consumers.

Marketing of Coconut—Systems and Practices

Village traders, in the primary market, collect coconuts from the growers. Majority of the growers, prefer to sell their produce to the village traders because the village traders operate in the interior areas close to them, which facilitates personal contacts. Besides, they provide advance money to the growers, on condition, that the produce should be sold to them only. They assemble the produce purchased from the growers and pass them to the wholesalers in the assembling market.

Primary village traders operate in the assembling market. The wholesalers purchase coconuts both from the village traders and growers. Growers, having more stock and good holding capacity, directly contact the wholesalers and sell their produce. They are in a position to take advantage of the better price offers. The wholesalers do not hold coconut stock for a long period. They transport the stock to the terminal market in Vadasery, as soon as they accumulate enough stock for a full trucker load. At Vadasery, the wholesalers deposit the coconut in the godown of commission agents and entrust the task of selling the coconuts to them. The commission agents make an advance of about 60 per cent to 80 per cent of the market value of the coconuts deposited by the wholesalers. The commission agents do not charge interest on this advance, if the sale is effected within 3 days. If the stock remains unsold for more than 3 days, interest is charged, for the excess period. The duration of the interest-free stocking period and rate of interest charged normally depend on the business relations that exist between them. The commission agents have to locate suitable buyers with price offers that are acceptable to their clients. The buyers are either exporters or secondary wholesalers. The commission agents get a commission for their services.

The wholesalers operate in the terminal market at Vadasery. They generally make use of the services of brokers to purchase coconut. The brokers contact the commission agents and purchase the quantity required by the secondary wholesalers. The brokers are paid brokerage for the services rendered by them. The wholesalers sell the produce to the retailers at Vadasery and also send coconuts to the wholesalers, located mostly at places like Delhi, Chennai, Madurai, Mumbai, Kolkatta, Kanpur, Indore, Amritsar, Nagpur, and Hyderabad.

Marketing Channels

In this section, an attempt is made to identify the channels of distribution for coconut in the Kanyakumari District of Tamil Nadu.

The flow chart given in figure 6.1 shows the different participants in the marketing channels.

The different marketing channels, identified in the marketing of coconut in the study area are given below.

Chart 6.1. Marketing Channels for Coconut

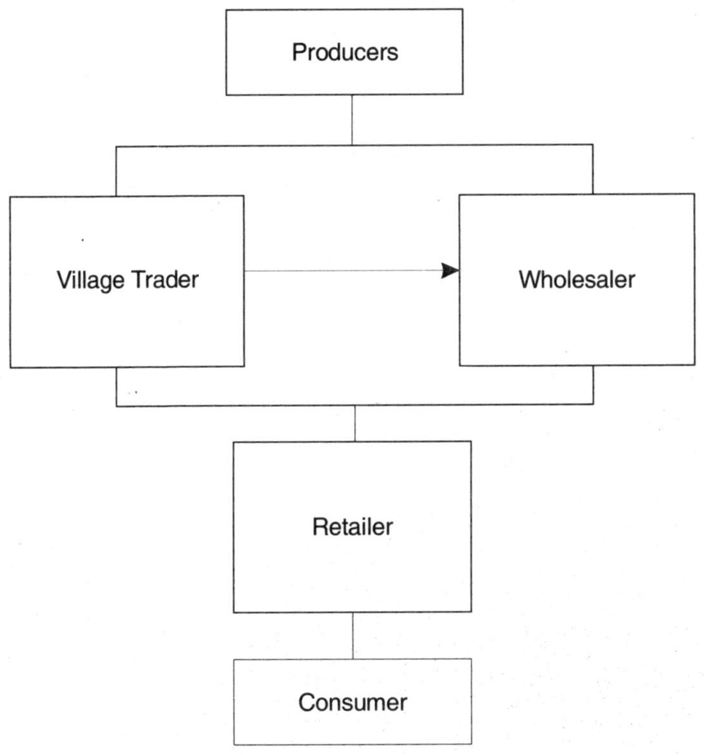

Channel I : Producer—Village trader—Wholesaler—Retailer—Consumer

Channel II : Producer—Wholesaler—Retailer—Consumer

Channel III : Producer—Village trader—Retailer—Consumer

Marketable Surplus

Marketable surplus is that quantity of the produce which can be made available to the non-farming population of the country. In other words, marketable surplus is the estimated quantity to be marketed by the producer, after making some provisions for meeting his own family consumption, farm requirements and social and religious requirements. In this section, an attempt is made to analyse the marketable surplus of the sample growers.

Marketable surplus is estimated by using the following equation:

$Ms = Qp - Qr$

where,

Ms = Marketable surplus

Qp = Quantity of coconut produced

Qr = Quantity of coconut retained for family consumption and free gifts.

The production, retention and marketable surplus of the sample growers, producing coconut, are shown in Table 6.1.

Table 6.1. The Marketable Surplus of Coconut

Sl. No.	Particulars	Marginal farmers		Small farmers		Large farmers	
		Quantity* (in 1000 nuts)	%	Quantity* (in 1000 nuts)	%	Quantity* (in 1000 nuts)	%
1.	Number of Coconuts Produced	1019.665	100.00	1398.133	100.00	2873.3	100.00
2.	Quantity of Coconuts Retained	8.667	0.85	11.45	0.79	17.814	0.62
3.	Marketable Surplus	1010.998	99.15	1387.088	99.21	2855.486	99.38

Source: Primary Data

*The aggregate for the sample farmers for the year 2008-09

It is observed from Table 6.1, that the percentage of marketable surplus to the total quantity of coconut produced by the marginal farmers, worked out to 99.15 per cent. Hence, it is inferred from the above analysis, that the sample marginal farmers retained only less than one per cent of their produce for meeting their family and other requirements.

It is also observed from Table 6.1, that the percentage of marketable surplus to the total quantity of coconut produced by the small farmers, worked out to 99.21 per cent. So it is inferred from the above analysis that the sample small farmers retained only less than one per cent of their coconut production for meeting their family and other requirements.

It is inferred from Table 6.1 that the percentage of marketable surplus to the total quantity of coconut produced by the large farmers worked out to 99.38 per cent. Thus the analysis reveals that the sample large farmers retained only less than one per cent of their coconut production, for meeting their family and other requirements.

Storage of Coconut

Storage of coconut is very essential element, in a study on marketing because it would help avoiding post-harvest glut in the market and the resulting low price on account of immediate sale. The more affluent growers, store their coconuts expecting a better price later. An analysis on storage of coconut, was carried out and the results are presented in Table 6.2 *(See on next page)*.

It is observed from Table 6.2, that out of the 26 marginal farmers who stored coconut, 12 growers stored coconut for a period up to 15 days, 8 growers for a period of 15 to 30 days and only 6 growers stored coconut for a period between 30 to 45 days. The table also reveals that the sample marginal farmers stored 23.50 per cent of the marketable surplus.

It is derived from Table 6.2, that out of the 24 small farmers who stored coconut, 13 growers stored coconut for a period between 15 to 30 days, 6 for a period of 30 to 45 days and only 4 growers stored coconut for a period up to 15 days. The table also reveals that the sample small farmers stored 36.78 per cent of the marketable surplus.

It is observed from Table 6.2, that out of the 25 large farmers who stored coconut, 10 growers stored coconut for a period between 15 to 30 days, 9 for a period of 30 to 45 days and only 6 stored coconut for a period up to 15 days. The table also reveals that the sample large farmers stored 53.94 per cent of the marketable surplus.

Table 6.2. Storage of Coconut by the Sample Farmers

Sl. No.	Number of Days stored	Marginal farmers		Small farmers		Large farmers	
		Number of farmers	Quantity (in 1000 nuts)	Number of farmers	Quantity (in 1000 nuts)	Number of farmers	Quantity (in 1000 nuts)
1.	Up to 15	12	114.872 (48.35)	4	85.454 (16.75)	6	190.991 (12.40)
2.	15 to 30	8	76.479 (32.19)	13	291.410 (57.12)	10	806.628 (52.37)
3.	30 to 45	6	46.234 (19.46)	6	133.307 (26.13)	9	542.630 (35.23)
	Total stored	26	237.585	24	510.171	25	1540.249
	Marketable Surplus	1010.998		1387.088		2855.486	
	Percentage of coconut stored to marketable surplus	23.50		36.78		53.94	

Source: Primary data
Figures in parenthesis denotes percentages to total

Storage Loss

Usually, coconut is heaped in a store room in the grower's own farm houses. Only a limited number of them stored their produce for more than two months. The place of storage and also the period of storage, influenced the storage loss. It was found that out of 2,37,585 coconuts stored by the marginal farmers, 2351 coconuts were lost in storage. The percentage of storage loss to the quantity of coconut stored, worked out to 0.99 per cent, which was less than one per cent of the quantity stored.

It was revealed that out of 5,10,171 coconuts stored by the small farmers, 4335 coconuts were lost in storage. The percentage of storage loss to the quantity of coconuts stored, worked out to 0.85 per cent, which was less than one per cent of the quantity stored.

It was found that out of 15,40,249 coconuts stored by the large farmers, 11,088 coconuts were lost in storage. The percentage of storage loss to the quantity of coconuts stored worked out to 0.71 per cent, which was less than one per cent of the quantity stored.

Marketed Surplus

Marketed Surplus is the difference between marketable surplus and the storage loss. It is that quantity of the produce which the grower actually sells in the market. In the study area, it was observed that the sample growers sold their produce within one year and no case of carry-over stock was reported. In the present study, marketed surplus is estimated by using the following equation:

$$Mds = Ms - Qi$$

where,

Mds = Marketed Surplus

Ms = Marketable Surplus

Qi = Quantity of coconut lost in storage

Table 6.3 shows the marketed surplus of coconut among the sample growers.

It is observed from Table 6.3, that the percentage of marketed surplus to the marketable surplus worked out to 99.77 in the case of marginal farmers. It implies that only 0.23 per cent of the marketable surplus was lost in storage. It is also observed from the table that the percentage of marketed surplus to the marketable surplus worked out to 99.69 in the case of small farmers. It implies that only 0.31 per cent of the marketable surplus was lost in storage. It is derived from the table, that the percentage of marketed surplus to the marketable surplus worked out to 99.61 in the case of large farmers. It implies that only 0.39 per cent of the marketable surplus was lost in storage.

Table 6.3. Marketed Surplus of Coconut

Sl. No.	Particulars	Marginal farmers (in 1000 nuts)	Small farmers (in 1000 nuts)	Large farmers (in 1000 nuts)
1.	Marketable surplus	1010.998	1387.088	2855.486
2.	Number of nuts lost in storage	2.351	4.335	11.088
3.	Marketed surplus	1008.647	1382.753	2844.398
4.	Percentage of marketed surplus to marketable surplus	99.77	99.69	99.61

Source: Primary Data

Disposal of Marketed Surplus

In the study area, the average quantity of coconut sold in a year and the different types of middlemen, through whom sales were effected by the sample farmers are furnished in Table 6.4.

It is observed from Table 6.4, that out of 80 sample marginal coconut farmers, 76.25 per cent of the farmers sold their produce to the village traders, and 23.75 per cent of them to the whole salers. The village traders also allow the producers to run up a credit with their business, on the condition that they should sell their produce only to them.

It could also be observed from the table, that the growers sold 799.151 thousands of coconut through village traders which accounted for 79.23 per cent of the total marketed surplus. About 24 per cent of the growers sold 20.77 per cent of the marketed surplus through wholesalers. This shows that growers having relatively more stock, sell their produce to the wholesalers to take advantage of better prices. Marginal farmers sold 79.23 per cent of their produces to village traders and small farmers sold 71.28 per cent to village traders whereas large farmers sold only 58 per cent of their produces to village traders. This shows that growers are more interested in selling their produce to local traders. Easy accessibility and advance money received by the growers from the local traders, are the major reasons for more sales through the village traders.

Table 6.4. Disposal of Marketed Surplus

Sl. No.	Sources of sales	Marginal farmers		Small farmers		Large farmers	
		Number of farmers	Quantity (in 1000 nuts)	Number of farmers	Quantity (in 1000 nuts)	Number of farmers	Quantity (in 1000 nuts)
1.	Village traders	61 (76.25)	799.151 (79.23)	40 (66.34)	985.626 (71.28)	20.984 (52)	1651.173 (58.05)
2.	Wholesalers	19 (23.75)	209.496 (20.77)	20 (33.66)	397.127 (28.72)	19.016 (23.75)	1193.225 (41.95)
3.	Total	80 (100.00)	1008.647 (100.00)	60 (100.00)	1382.753 (100.00)	80 (100.00)	2844.398 (100.00)
	Marketed Surplus		1008.67		1382.753		2844.398

Source: Primary Data

Figures in parenthesis denote percentage to total marketed surplus

Cost of Marketing Coconut

Marketing functions add value to the produce to be sold but they also involve costs which have ultimate impact on the profitability of the sellers. The cost involved in transporting the coconut from the point of production to the point of consumption, known otherwise as the cost of performing marketing functions, is discussed in this section.

Marketing Cost of Producer

The coconut producers, in the study area, sold their produce through different channels. The cost incurred by them in marketing one thousand coconuts through different marketing channels was worked out and the results are presented in Table 6.5.

Table 6.5. Cost Incurred by the Producers in Marketing of Coconut

Sl. No.	Particulars	Channel I		Channel II		Average	
		Cost (₹ per 1000 nuts)	%	Cost (₹ per 1000 nuts)	%	Cost (₹ per 1000 nuts)	%
1.	Transportation cost	23	25.56	23	17.69	23	20.91
2.	Commission/ brokerage	12	13.33	50	38.46	31	28.18
3.	Tax and village mahimai	25	27.78	25	19.23	25	22.73
4.	Storage loss	20	22.22	15	11.54	17.5	15.91
5.	Loading and Unloading	10	11.11	17	13.08	13.5	12.27
	Total	**90**	**100.00**	**130**	**100.00**	**110**	**100.00**

Source: Primary Data

It is observed from Table 6.5, that the cost incurred by the producers in marketing one thousand coconuts, worked out to ₹ 90 in Channel I and ₹ 130 in Channel II with an overall average of ₹ 110 per thousand coconuts.

Among the various costs in marketing coconut in Channel I, the tax and village mahamai charged, had a major share of 27.78 per cent in the total marketing cost, followed by cost of transportation constituting 25.56 per cent. Both these items constituted 53.34 per cent of the total marketing cost. The cost of storage loss accounted for 22.22 per cent, which formed the third major item, in the total marketing cost.

The commission/brokerage charge occupy a major share in Channel II and accounted for 38.46 per cent of the total marketing cost, followed by the amount of tax and village mahimai constituting 19.23 per cent. The transportation charges worked out to 17.69 per cent which was the third major item. Both commission/brokerage and tax and village mahimai together constituted 57.69 per cent of the total marketing cost. The same cost worked out to 41.11 per cent in Channel I and thus the producer got the advantage of reduction in marketing cost by about 10 per cent in Channel II. This was because, the producers sold their produce directly to the wholesalers. The cost of loading and unloading was 13.08 per cent which was 1.97 per cent more when compared to Channel I, because the producers had to load and unload their produce to bring it to the market.

The comparative analysis revealed that the commission/ brokerage incurred by the producer in marketing coconut, was the maximum when the average is taken into account. This cost was followed by tax and village mahamai and transportation cost, which were more in Channel I. Loading and unloading charges were the least in both the Channels but were comparatively high in Channel II.

Marketing Cost Incurred by Village Traders

The details of marketing cost incurred by the village traders in marketing thousand coconuts was worked out and the results obtained are presented in Table 6.6.

It is observed from Table 6.6, that the marketing cost incurred by the village traders was ₹ 373 per thousand coconuts. Among the different components of marketing cost incurred, rejection and weight loss formed a major share of 38.08 per cent, followed by transportation cost with 21.18 per cent and establishment and administration cost with 19.57 per cent. These three costs, put together, constituted 78.83 per cent of the total marketing cost incurred by the village traders. The other expenses incurred by the village traders, like loading and unloading worked out to 11.80 per cent and incidental charges and weighment and packaging, each with

1.34 per cent respectively. The share of expenditure on husking was 6.70 per cent.

Table 6.6. Cost Incurred by the Village Traders in Marketing Coconut

Sl. No.	Cost Components	Cost (₹ Per 1000 nuts)	Percentage
1.	Transport	79	21.18
2.	Husking	25	6.70
3.	Loading and Unloading	44	11.80
4.	Weighment and Packaging	5	1.34
5.	Rejection and Weight Loss	142	38.08
6.	Establishment and Administration	73	19.57
7.	Incidental Charges	5	1.34
	Total	**373**	**100**

Source: Primary Data

Marketing Cost of Wholesalers

The details of cost incurred by the wholesalers in marketing coconut were estimated and the results obtained are presented in Table 6.7.

It is observed from Table 6.7, that the marketing cost incurred by the wholesalers was ₹ 430 per thousand coconuts. Among the different components of marketing cost incurred, rejection and weight loss formed a major share of 39.77 per cent, followed by establishment and administration cost with 16.74 per cent and transportation cost with 16.28 per cent. These three costs, put together, constituted 72.79 per cent of the total marketing cost incurred by the wholesalers. The share of expenditure on husking was 5.35 per cent. The other expenses incurred by the wholesalers, like loading and unloading, worked out to 9.07 per cent, market fee constituted 10 per cent and weighment and packaging 2.79 per cent. These three costs, put together, constituted 21.86 per cent of the total marketing cost incurred by the wholesalers.

Table 6.7. Cost Incurred by the Wholesalers in Marketing Coconut

Sl. No.	Cost Components	Cost (₹ Per 1000 nuts)	Percentage
1.	Transport	70	16.28
2.	Husking	23	5.35
3.	Loading and Unloading	39	9.07
4.	Weighment and Packaging	12	2.79
5.	Rejection and Weight Loss	171	39.77
6.	Establishment and Administration	72	16.74
7.	Market Fee	43	10.00
	Total	**430**	**100**

Source: Primary Data

Marketing Cost Incurred by Retailer

The cost incurred by the retailers in marketing coconut is given in Table 6.8.

Table 6.8. Cost incurred by the Retailers in Marketing Coconut

Sl. No.	Cost Components	Cost (₹ Per 1000 nuts)	Percentage
1.	Transport	60	31.41
2.	Loading and Unloading	10	5.24
3.	Rejection and Weight Loss	95	49.74
4.	Establishment and administration	21	10.99
5.	Incidental charges	5	2.62
	Total	**191**	**100**

Source: Primary Data

Table 6.8 reveals, that among the various costs incurred by the retailers, rejection and weight loss had a major share of 49.74 per cent of the total marketing cost. Cost of transportation was the second major item accounting for 31.41 per cent, followed by establishment and administration cost which accounted for 10.99 per cent. The loading and unloading charges and the incidental charges accounted for 5.24 per cent and 2.62 per cent respectively. It could be inferred that marketing cost incurred by the retailers was the lowest when compared to the cost incurred by other intermediaries. This may be due to non-payment of commission and storage charges.

Price-Spread in Coconut Trade

The difference between the price paid by the consumer and the price received by the producer for an equivalent quantity is known as 'price spread'. The study of price-spread in coconut marketing, is an important aspect, since it reflects the share of the producer and different market functionaries as well as the cost of marketing, met from the price paid by the consumer. The price-spread varies, depending on the number of intermediaries involved in the marketing channel. Hence, more the number of intermediaries, higher is the price-spread and vice-versa. Generally, the channel having the lowest price-spread is preferred. The price-spread is one of the important factors which will have a decisive impact on the profit margin of the producers. Hence a study on the price-spread becomes important. The costs incurred and margin earned by the various market intermediaries, in different channels, in the process of marketing of coconut per quintal, in the study area, are presented in Table 6.9.

It could be observed from Table 6.9, that the producer's share in the price paid by consumer is estimated to be around 80 per cent in all the three channels in the study area. It implies that there is not much difference in the net price received by the producer whatever may be the type of channel he chooses

Table 6.9. Price-spread for Coconut

Sl.No.	Particulars	Channel I		Channel II		Channel III	
		Amount (₹ per 1000 nuts)	%	Amount (₹ per 1000 nuts)	%	Amount (₹ per 1000 nuts)	%
1.0	**Producer**						
1.1	Net Price Received	5470	78.55	5770	82.85	5470	78.55
1.2	Marketing Cost	90	1.29	130	1.87	90	1.29
1.3	Gross Price Received	5560	79.84	5900	84.72	5560	79.84
2.0	**Village Trader**						
2.1	Price Paid	5560	79.84			5560	79.84
2.2	Marketing Cost	373	5.36			373	5.36
2.3	Marketing Margin	120	1.72			320	4.60
2.4	Price Received	6053	86.92			6253	89.79
3.0	**Wholesaler**						
3.1	Price Paid	6053	86.92	5900	84.72		
3.2	Marketing Cost	430	6.17	430	6.17		
3.3	Marketing Margin	100	1.44	253	3.63		
3.4	Price Received	6583	94.53	6583	94.53		
4.0	**Retailer**						
4.1	Price Paid	6583	94.53	6583	94.53	6253	89.79
4.2	Marketing Cost	191	2.74	191	2.74	191	2.74
4.3	Marketing Margin	190	2.73	190	2.73	520	7.47
4.4	Price Received (or) price paid by Consumer	6964	100	6964	100.00	6954	100.00

Source: Primary Data

to market his produce. It is observed, that the producer's share is the maximum in Channel II, which is 82.85 per cent, followed by the other two Channels each constituting 78.55 per cent of the price paid by consumers. This is due to the fact that the producer directly sells his produce to the village traders. The net share of the producer is found to be equal in the other two Channels because of more marketing costs incurred by the producer.

The marketing costs incurred by the producer are lower in Channel I and III, compared to Channel II, because of the absence of commission charges in the former. The marketing cost incurred by the village trader accounts for 5.36 per cent of the consumer price which was found to be the same among all the intermediaries. This was due to sales tax incurred by him.

The wholesaler earned a margin of 1.44 per cent of the consumer price when he purchased coconut directly from the producer, whereas it was 1.72 per cent when he purchased from the village traders. Thus, both the channels were found to be more beneficial to the producer as well as to the wholesaler.

Price-spread analysis shows that, both Channel I and III are best from the producers' point of view. However, the producer prefers retailers. Between Channels I and II, Channel II is more profitable to the producer.

Overview of Channels with their Price-Spread

In order to identify the channel having the lowest price-spread, comparison was made among the different channels and the details are presented in Table 6.10.

Table 6.10 reveals, that price-spread in Channel II is the lowest, with ₹ 1194 per 1000 nuts because of less marketing cost and higher producer's price. The producer's price was the maximum in Channel II with ₹ 5770 per 1000 coconuts followed by ₹ 5470 per 1000 coconuts in Channels I and III.

The price-spread in Channel I and III, was the highest among all channels because of the existence of more number of marketing intermediaries and higher marketing cost.

Table 6.10. Price-spread under Different Channels

(Rupees per 1000 nuts)

Sl.No.	Particulars	Channels		
		I	II	III
1.	Consumer price	6964	6964	6964
2.	Producer's Price	5470	5770	5470
3.	Price-spread	1494	1194	1494
4.	Marketing Cost	1084	751	654
5.	Marketing Margin	410	443	840

Source: Primary Data

Marketing Efficiency

The marketing efficiency refers to the effectiveness or competence with which a market structure performs its designated function. Marketing efficiency is directly related to the cost involved in transporting goods from the producer to the consumer and the quantity of service offered. A reduction in marketing cost, without reduction in consumer satisfaction, indicates improvement in efficiency. A higher level of consumer satisfaction, at higher marketing cost, might have increased efficiency, if the additional satisfaction derived by consumer, outweighs the additional cost incurred on the marketing process. But a change that reduces cost as well as consumer satisfaction need not indicate increase in marketing efficiency. In the present study, the marketing efficiency of the different channels, has been studied using Shepherd's Method and Composite Index Method.

Shepherd's Method

The economic efficiency of the marketing system can be measured as the ratio of the consumer price per unit of coconut to the marketing cost per unit. The higher the ratio, the higher is the efficiency of the marketing system.

In order to assess the marketing efficiency in the sale of coconut, Shepherd's[2] Formula in the following form is used

$$ME = \frac{V}{I} - 1,$$

where,

V = Value of Produce sold (or) Consumer price per unit of coconut

I = Total marketing cost (or) Marketing cost per unit.

ME = Marketing Efficiency

The marketing efficiency of the different channels is worked out using Shepherd's Method and the results obtained are furnished in Table 6.11.

Table 6.11. Marketing Efficiency Analysis using Shepherd's Method

Sl.No.	Particulars	Channel I	Channel II	Channel III
1.	Consumer Price (V) (₹ Per 1000 nuts.)	6954	6964	6964
2.	Total Marketing Cost (I) (₹ Per 1000 nuts.)	1084	751	654
3.	Marketing Efficiency	5.42	8.27	9.65

Source: Primary Data

Table 6.11 reveals, that among the three channels, Channel III is found to be the most efficient. The efficiency index for Channel III is the maximum with 9.65, followed by Channel II with 8.27. The marketing efficiency in Channel III is better than in the remaining two channels because of less marketing cost.

Decision Behaviour

Coconut is considered to be the most important and useful tree among the tropical palms. It has been in cultivation in India from time immemorial. It perhaps yields more products of use to mankind than any other tree. Each and every part of the coconut palm is used in India, in one way or other and the Classics of India have rightly eulogized it as *'Kalpavriksha'* owing to its multifarious uses of our daily life. Though it is evenly cultivated, the cultivators face many problems. Another important problem faced by the growers is connected with the sale of coconut. The coconut growers in the study area were left with two options while marketing their produce. The first option was selling coconut to the village traders and the second one was selling through wholesalers. The factors that influenced the growers to select a particular medium, are analysed by making use of Garrett's Ranking Technique and the results are discussed below.

Problems faced by the Farmers in Coconut Cultivation

Most of the farmers in the study area face many problems relating to the cultivation of coconut in their farms. They include Incidence of pests and diseases, High cost of input, Lack of irrigation, Shortage of tree climbers and Lack of scientific knowledge. The various problems faced by the farmers in coconut cultivation are analysed and presented in Table 6.12.

Farmers are operating in the production centres. The growers can sell their produce on any day and at any time to the village traders. It is evident from Table 6.12 that 'incidence of pests and diseases' is the major problem in coconut cultivation, faced by the village farmers with a mean score of 56.36. When the farmers want to produce more by applying the latest technology, they have to incur high cost of input which ranked as the second vital problem faced by the coconut cultivators with a mean score of 54.67. Many a time the monsoons fail and leads to reduction in yield due to lack of proper irrigation facilities and this factor ranked third with a mean score of 47.18. 'Shortage of tree climbers' ranked fourth, with a mean score of 42.00 followed by 'lack of scientific knowledge among the cultivators' ranking the last, with the least mean score of 39.92.

Table 6.12. Problems Faced by the Farmers in Coconut Cultivation

Sl.No.	Problems	Garrett's Mean Score	Rank
1.	Incidence of pests and diseases	56.36	I
2.	High cost of input	54.67	II
3.	Lack of irrigation facilities	47.18	III
4.	Shortage of tree climbers	42.00	IV
5.	Lack of scientific knowledge	39.92	V

Source: Primary Data

Problems faced by the Farmers in Marketing Coconut

It is a common phenomenon that, many a time the farmers are put to hardships in marketing their produce in the markets where they can get better price. An attempt has been made to identify the problems faced by the growers in marketing coconut. They include Price fluctuation, Absence of cooperative society, Lack of market information, In-adequate storage facility and Exploitation by middlemen. The identified problems of growers in the marketing of coconut are ranked by making use of Garrett's Ranking Technique and the details are presented in Table 6.13.

It could be observed from Table 6.13, that price fluctuation is the major problem faced by the growers with a mean score of 55.09. Growers could not get the right price for their produce in the assembling market, which is far away from the production centres. They have to incur more transportation cost and spend more time. Therefore, they feel that they cannot enjoy price benefits in other markets. There is absence of Cooperative Societies in the study area also. Hence, 'absence of Cooperative Society' is the second important problem with a mean score of 48.35. 'Lack of Market Information' is the third important factor with a mean score of 44.37. Usually, coconut is stored in the grower's own house, which is normally unhygienic. This results in deterioration in quality and weight loss and thus they do not fetch a reasonable price. Thus, 'inadequate storage facility' is the fourth important problem with a mean score of 41.25. 'Exploitation by middlemen' is found to be the least important problem faced by the growers in the study area, with the lowest mean score of 37.17.

Table 6.13. Problems Faced by the Producers in Marketing Coconut

Sl.No.	Factor	Garrett's Mean Score	Rank
1.	Price fluctuation	55.09	I
2.	Absence of Cooperative society	45.35	II
3.	Lack of Market Information	44.37	III
4.	Inadequate Storage Facility	41.25	IV
5.	Exploitation by Middlemen	37.17	V

Source: Primary Data

Price Analysis

Coconut, being an agricultural, exportable and consumable commodity, its price always depends on the international demand and supply position. As production and supply of coconut in the world market are widely fluctuating, world prices of coconut have always fluctuated, which are reflected in the domestic prices also. Like other commodities, prices of coconut too have year-wise and season wise variations. Hence, an attempt has been made to analyse the variations in the price of coconut.

The Analytical Framework

Time series analysis was carried out to study the pattern of price variation of coconut over a period of time. A multiplicative model of the following type has been used.

$Y = T \times C \times S \times I$,

where

Y = Actual price in rupees per quintal

T = Secular Trend

C = Cyclical Variation

S = Seasonal Variation

I = Irregular Variation

In the present study, due to non availability of monthly average price statistics over years, the components were decomposed into three categories namely, Secular Trend, Cyclical Variation and Irregular Variation. The seasonal variation was separately analysed with ten years' monthly data.

Secular Trend

The secular trend is the basic tendency of prices to increase or decrease over a period of time. It describes the pattern of behaviour which has characterized the series in the past. In the present study, the trend of time series of prices was worked out, with linear regression equation, since the prices exhibited linear relationship with time. A trend equation fitted for the coconut is as follows:

$$Y = a + bt,$$

where,

Y = Price of coconut rupees per quintal

a = Constant

b = Regression co-efficient

t = Time in years

Cyclical Variation

A careful study of cyclical variation, facilitates to face recession period and to reap the benefits during booms. In the present study, the cyclical variations in the annual prices of coconut, were studied through Moving Average Method. The steps involved are shown below:

Step 1 : Dividing the actual average yearly price by trend price.

Step 2 : Computation of six yearly centered moving averages for the detrended data which formed cyclical variations.

Seasonal Variation

It is a variation, which occurs with some degree of regularity within a specific period of one year or shorter. This study is useful to take useful policy decisions regarding purchase, production, inventory control and the like. In the present study, the seasonal variations in the monthly average prices were studied for ten years, by applying the Moving Average Method. The steps involved are shown below:

Step 1 : Computation of 12 months' moving averages, for monthly average price series of coconut.

Step 2 : Obtaining the percentage series of actual prices to moving average prices and arranging them by month.

Step 3 : Calculating median for each month and eventually arriving at the seasonal (monthly) indices through adjustment factor.

Irregular Variations

It is the irregular movement of prices, over a period of time due to random factors. In the present study, Cyclical-Irregular (CI) components were derived, by dividing the actual time series with trend element since seasonal element was absent in the annual price series. This Cyclical-Irregular (CI) component was again divided by Cyclical Component to estimate the irregular variation.

Temporal Variation

A study on temporal variation of prices would be useful in forecasting the price movements in future. This would, in turn, help the producers and traders in making effective decision in production and marketing of coconut, including storage.

Kanyakumari is a major market for both domestic and international trade of coconut, in India. Moreover, this market has got the advantage of having good means of transportation in the form of, roads and railways. The price effect in Kanyakumri market will be reflected in all other markets. Therefore, Kanyakumari market was selected to study the temporal price variations of coconut.

The present study analyzed the temporal variations of coconut prices in Kanyakumari market, using average annual prices of coconut for the period from 1986-87 to 2005-06. Table 6.14 *(See on next page)* shows the trend, cyclical and irregular variations of prices of coconut in the Kanyakumari Market.

Secular Trend

Secular Trend is the basic tendency of prices to increase or decrease over a period of time. The concept does not include short-range oscillations in prices but the steady movements over a long time. To identify the trend in prices of coconut at Kanyakumari market for the period from 1986-87 to 2005-06, the linear regression equation was fitted and the estimated trend function was,

$$Y = 1696.105 + 92.04^{**}$$
$$(271.19) \quad (22.64)$$
$$R^2 = 0.479$$

Figures in parenthesis denote standard errors
** Significant at one percent level.

Table 6.14. Trend, Cyclical and Irregular Variations of Coconut Prices in Kanyakumari Market

Sl.No.	Year	Actual Price (₹ Per 1000 nuts)	Trend Price (₹ Per 1000 nuts)	Cyclical variation Index	Irregular variation Index
1.	1986-87	1508	1788		
2.	1987-88	1575	1880		
3.	1988-89	1583	1972		
4.	1989-90	1550	2064	0.84	0.89
5.	1990-91	1483	2156	0.90	0.76
6.	1991-92	2229	2248	0.97	1.02
7.	1992-93	2667	2340	1.03	1.10
8.	1993-94	3083	2432	1.12	1.13
9.	1994-95	2979	2524	1.22	0.97
10.	1995-96	2896	2617	1.24	0.89
11.	1996-97	3722	2709	1.19	1.16
12	1997-98	4225	2801	1.15	1.31
13.	1998-99	2542	2893	1.13	0.78
14.	1999-00	2667	2985	1.09	0.82
15.	2000-01	3375	3077	1.01	1.09
16.	2001-02	3000	3169	0.96	0.99
17.	2002-03	3325	3261	0.95	1.08
18.	2003-04	3083	3353		
19.	2004-05	3000	3445		
20.	2005-06	2758	3537		

Source: Computed Data

It could be observed from the above function, that the co-efficient of determination (R^2) was 0.479 which indicated that 47.90 per cent of variation in the price of coconut was explained by the dependent variable.

The results also show that there has been a significant increase in the price of coconut over the years. The annual average price of coconut per thousand nuts, has increased at the rate of ₹ 92.04 per annum. The actual price series with the estimated trend value is presented in Table 6.14 and is depicted in Figure 6.1.

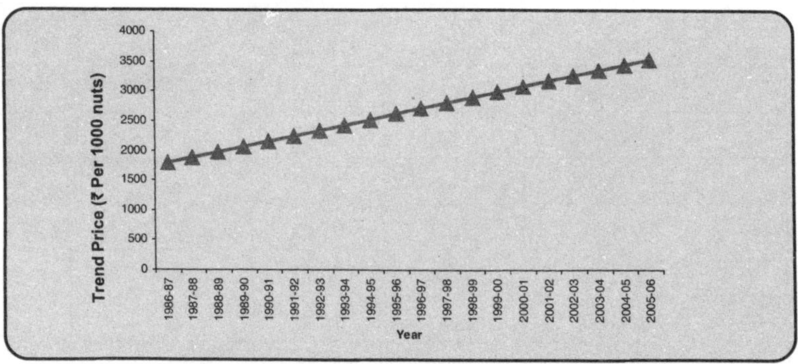

Fig. 6.1. Estimated Price Trend of Coconut during 1986-87 to 2005-06

Cyclical Variations

Cyclical variations in coconut price refers to the recurrent up and down movements around secular trend levels, which have

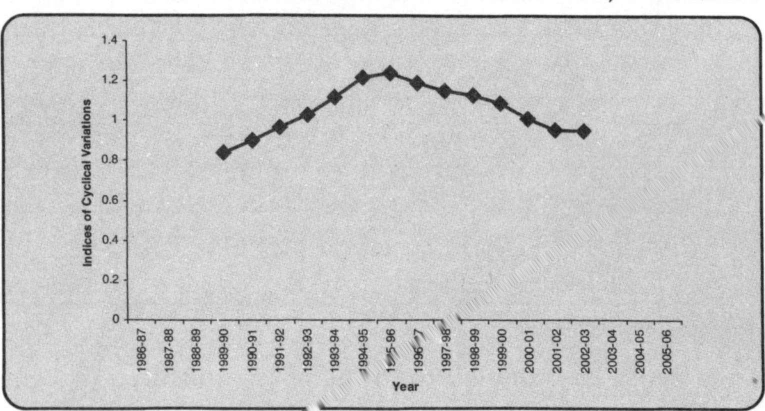

Fig. 6.2. Cyclical Variation in Prices of Coconut during 1986-87 to 2005-06

duration anywhere from 2 to 12 years. These cycles may or may not be periodic. This study is useful in framing suitable policies for stabilizing the price level. The cyclical variation in the prices of coconut is analyzed by using the average method. The results are presented in Table 6.14 and the indices of cyclical variations have been plotted in figure 6.2.

It could be seen from Table 6.14 that the indices of cyclical variation in the prices of coconut reached the maximum in 1995-96 and it started declining thereafter till the end of the study period.

Irregular Variations

Irregular Variation refers to such variations in the prices of coconut which do not repeat themselves in a definite pattern. Irregular variation in prices includes all types of variation other than the trend, seasonal and cyclical movements. Irregular variation in price is caused by certain special isolated occurrences such as sudden change in demand or rapid technological progress. By their nature, these movements are irregular and unpredictable. An analysis of irregular variation in the price of coconut, in Kanyakumari market was carried

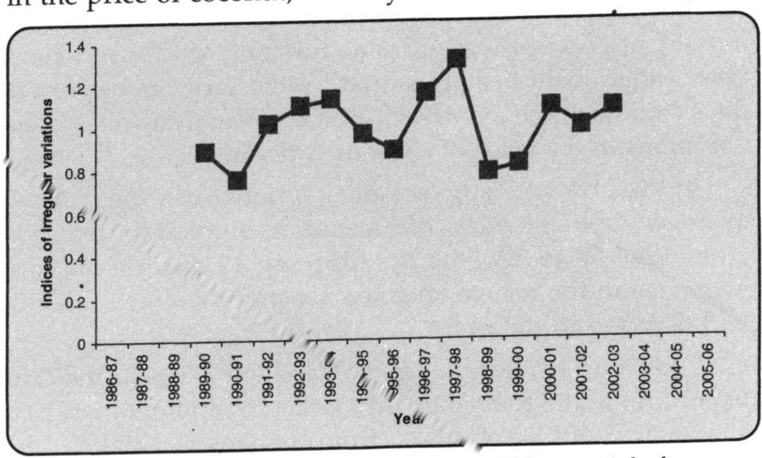

Fig. 6.3. Irregular Variations in Prices of Coconut during 1986-87 to 2005-06

out and the results obtained are presented in Table 6.14 and depicted in Figure 6.3.

It could be observed from Table 6.14, that once in six or seven years the price of coconut varied due to much irregular factors. The indices of irregular variations for the price of coconut in the Kanyakumari market ranged from 0.76 to 1.31. The co-efficient of variation of irregular variation is 16.53 per cent. Thus it is inferred from the table that irregular variations in the price of coconut was confirmed by the co-efficient of variation of the irregular indices. The irregular variations in the price of coconut may be due to the sudden changes in demand, influenced by the changes in the taste and buying behavior of the customers, the price of substitutes, change in relative income level and the like.

Seasonal Variation

Coconut, being a rain-fed crop, is subject to seasonal variation in prices. Seasonal variation in the prices of coconut was observed within a year due to its characteristic supply. Though consumption is in small quantity, coconut is being used daily. Hence, there exists a regular demand throughout the year. But the supply varies with the season of production. The harvest of coconut is regular and usually once in 45 days. Only small quantities are stored by the growers beyond 90 days from the time of harvest. Hence, an analysis of seasonal variations in the price of coconut is pertinent.

In the present study, seasonal variations in the monthly average wholesale prices of coconut are studied for ten years from 1996-97 to 2005-06 by applying 12 months moving average and the results obtained are presented in Table 6.15 and depicted in figure 6.4.

Table 6.15 reveals that much variation exists in the price of coconut in the Kanyakumari market in different months of a year. It could be observed from the seasonal indices that lower prices prevailed from April to October and January to March. This is due to the heavy arrivals, the monsoon and

Table 6.15. Average Seasonal Indices of Price of Coconut in Kanyakumari District during 1996-97 to 2005-06

Sl. No.	Month	Seasonal Index
1.	April	99.9
2.	May	97.9
3.	June	98.9
4.	July	99.7
5.	August	99.9
6.	September	100.3
7.	October	100.6
8.	November	101.6
9.	December	101.3
10.	January	99.7
11.	February	99.9
12.	March	99.9

Source: Computed Data

the post-harvest glut in the market. The lower prices in the months of April to October imply that the growers sold their produce after storing for some time. The highest price index between November and December was due to the shrinkage of arrivals and the prevalence of hot dry season.

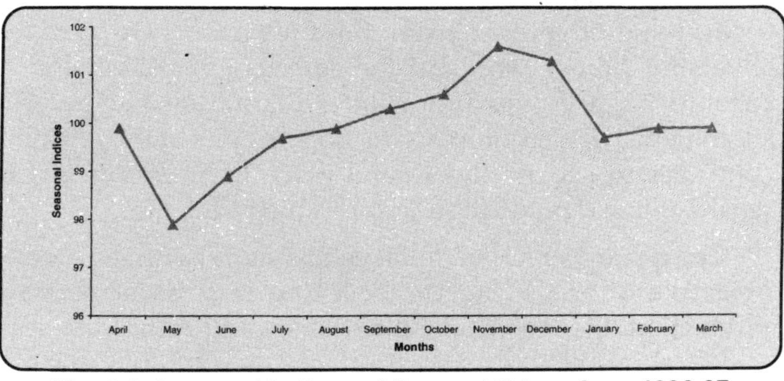

Fig. 6.4. Seasonal Indices of Coconut Prices from 1996-97 to 2005-06

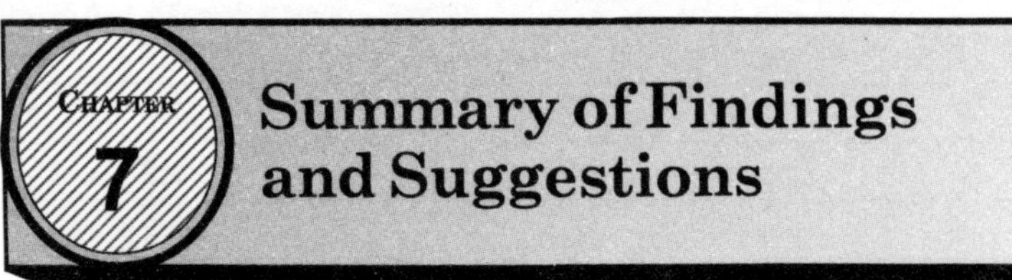

Summary of Findings and Suggestions

Introduction

Agriculture has continuously been playing a predominant role in the economic development of all developed and developing countries. Ever since India's independence, agriculture in India has taken major strides owing to the varietals and agronomic interventions of agricultural research and the resourcefulness of the farming community. Coconut is a multi-product crop and small and marginal farmers, involved in coconut growing, depend solely on this palm for their domestic requirements such as food, fuel and shelter.

Richly endowed with a favourable climate and soil condition, conducive to coconut cultivation, the Kanyakumari district offers scope for increasing production and productivity of coconut palm. But the farmers are attracted to raising rubber crop and the consequent conversion of coconut palm-groves into rubber plantation has given a stunning blow to coconut production. In spite of this, coconut continues to occupy the second place in importance with regard to area, production and productivity.

The researcher has undertaken this study, with the specific objective of analyzing the cost and returns of coconut production, the resource-use efficiency and returns to scale and evaluating the marketing cost, marketable margin, marketing margin, price spread and marketing efficiency of different channels of distribution in the domestic markets.

Besides studying the temporal variations in the price of coconut and assessing its total performance, the researcher has attempted to analyse the problems encountered in the cultivation and marketing of coconut by the growers. Appropriate suggestions on the basis of the findings have also been included.

In order to analyse and interpret both primary and secondary data, appropriate statistical tools such as Cobb-Duglas type function, Simple regression equation, Exponential function, Co-efficient of variation, Garrett's ranking technique, Capital budgeting techniques, Time Series analysis using multiplicative model and percentage analysis have been used.

Summary of Findings

Profile of the Study Area

Kanyakumari District was inaugurated on 1st November, 1959, with Nagercoil as its headquarters. The total area of the district is 1672 square miles and its population is 16,69,763. It is blessed with a favourable agro-climatic condition, for the growth of different varieties of crop. In the plains, semi-arid tropical monsoon type of climate prevails. The monsoon rains and the winter and summer rains account for the average annual rainfall of 1352.5mm. The annual average number of rainy days is normally 85.9. The major source of rainfall is the North-East monsoon. Besides the favourable climatic conditions of this district, the soil conditions constitute the physical basis for agriculture. Hence varieties of crops like food crops, plantain crops, cash crops, fibre crops and tuber crops are raised in the district.

Characteristics of the Sample Respondents

It is observed that among the total sample respondents selected for the study, there are 80 marginal farmers, 60 small and 40 large farmers. Of the respondents, a majority of the marginal and large farmers are in the age group of above 50 years. It is apparent from the study, that majority of the marginal, small and large farmers have 11-20 years experience in coconut cultivation and that the percentage of farmers with college level education is higher in all the three categories of farmers.

It is also found that agriculture is the occupation of majority of the sample respondents selected for the present study. A majority of 37.50 per cent marginal, 33.33 per cent small and 40.0 per cent large farmers have only four members in their family. It is understood that majority of the sample respondents have utilized one or two members in coconut cultivation.

World Production of Coconut

In terms of area under coconut cultivation among the major countries of the world cultivating coconut, the APCC countries occupy the first rank, with 10311.1 thousand hectares, followed by Africa ranking second with 526.7 thousand hectares, America ranking third with 468.45 thousand hectares, Asia ranking fourth with 82.6 thousand hectares and the Pacific countries ranking the last with 59.35 thousand hectares. The APCC countries contributed 89.75 per cent share of the total area, under coconut cultivation followed by Africa with 4.58 per cent, America with 4.08 per cent, and Asia with 0.72 per cent and the Pacific with 0.52 per cent, during the period of study.

The analysis of area under coconut cultivation among the world countries, has showed an increased rate of 1.84 per cent per annum during 1987-2006. It is also found that among the countries of the world, the area under coconut cultivation in the American coûntries, had increased at the rate of 12.93 per cent per annum and it had decreased at the rate of 3.66 per cent per annum in case of the Pacific countries. On the whole, the rate of variation in the area of coconut cultivation in the world countries was 4.99 per cent.

Among the major countries on world production of coconuts, the APCC countries occupied the first rank with 4,47,41,932.5 thousand nuts followed by the American countries in the second rank with 43,30,133.7 thousand nuts, Africa ranking third with 22,71,757 thousand nuts, Asia ranking fourth with 7,10,004.6 thousand nuts and the Pacific countries ranking fifth with 32,75,444.75 thousand nuts.

The analysis of world production of coconuts, among the world countries has revealed an increased rate of 3.73 per cent per annum. It has also been observed that among the countries of the world, the production of coconuts in the Asian countries, had increased at the rate of 9.17 per cent per annum and a decrease at the rate of 1.18 per cent per annum is seen in the case of African countries.

Co-efficients of variation, regarding the world production of coconuts has revealed that the Asian countries had recorded a maximum variation of 26.46 per cent, whereas Africa showed a minimum variation of 5.12 per cent. On the whole, the rate of variation in coconut cultivation in the world countries, during the period of study was 9.70 per cent.

America occupied the first rank with 8,975.909 nuts per hectare, among the major countries on world productivity of coconuts. Production was the least in the African countries, which ranked fifth, with 4,019.318 nuts per hectare.

During 2005, America had the highest productivity of 9,766.15 nuts per hectare, followed by Asia with 8,246 nuts per hectare, the Pacific countries with 6,961.08 nuts per hectare, APCC Countries with 4,641.32 nuts per hectare and Africa with the lowest productivity of 3,390.91 nuts per hectare.

The analysis of world productivity of coconuts, among the world countries, has shown an increase at the rate of 1.85 per cent per annum. It had increased in the Pacific countries and in the APCC countries at the rate of 3.30 per cent per annum. But it had decreased at the rate of 7.82 per cent per annum in the African countries. It had experienced a variation of 6.67 per cent. There was also a maximum variation of 32.85 per cent in the American countries. On the whole, the rate of variation in coconut productivity in the world countries, during the period of study was 5.14 per cent.

It is interesting to note that among the countries of the world, the APCC countries have stood first in terms of area of cultivation and production of coconut. Regarding productivity, America had stood first.

Coconut in APCC Countries

Analysis of coefficient of variation recorded a maximum variation of 21.43 per cent in Thailand where as in Philippines, it was recorded as 8.14 per cent. On the whole, the rate of variation in coconut production in the APCC countries, during the period of study was 9.34 per cent.

Production of Coconut in India

It is found that the production of coconut in India showed a significant increasing trend from a minimum of 6376.8 million nuts in 1986-87 to a maximum of 14811.1 million nuts in 2005-06 and the trend value also increased from 8498.903 million nuts in 1986-87 to 14377.23 million nuts in 2005-06. The area under coconut cultivation in India was the highest in 2005-06 and the lowest in 1988-87. The area under coconut cultivation has gone up from 1231.1 hectares in 1986-87 to 1946.8 hectares in 2005-06. It is also found that the trend value for area under coconut cultivation had increased from 1364.111 hectares in 1986-87 to 2036.819 hectares in 2005-06. It is also inferred that the yield of coconut per hectare had registered a fluctuating trend during the period of study.

It is observed that the productivity of coconut per hectare has registered an increase from 5179 nuts to 7760 nuts during the study period. It had increased from 6178.214 nuts in 1986-87 to 7180.086 nuts in 2005-06. The analysis of coconut production in India reveals a significant increase of 7.10 per cent per annum during the period under review. The area as well as productivity had also increased by 5.12 per cent and 1.98 per cent per annum respectively. Thus, it is observed that the increase in production was the result of increase in both area of cultivation and productivity.

Coefficients of variation revealed that India recorded 12.56 per cent variation in coconut production, during the period of study. The variation in productivity was 11.08 per cent whereas it was 6.24 per cent in the case of area under coconut cultivation.

Production of Coconut in Tamil Nadu

It is observed from the study that production of coconut in Tamil Nadu, had shown a fluctuating trend from 1986-87 to 2005-06. The trend value for production of coconut has increased from 2127.777 million nuts in 1986-89 to 4103.373 million nuts in 2005-06. It is also observed that the area under coconut cultivation in Tamil Nadu which was 174875 hectares in 1986-87 has increased tremendously to 370515 hectares in 2005-06. It is also inferred that the trend value for area under coconut cultivation in Tamil Nadu had also increased from 199726.1 hectares in 1986-87 to 378981.5 hectares in 2005-06. It is found that the yield of coconut per hectare in Tamil Nadu, had registered a fluctuating trend during the period of study.

The productivity of coconut per hectare ranged between 7260 nuts and 76117 nuts per hectare during the period 1986-87 to 2005-06. During the over all study period, there had been an increase in the production of coconut by 9.30 per cent per annum. Analysis of area of coconut cultivation showed an increase by 8.37 per cent per annum and increase in productivity by 0.93 per cent per annum. Thus, it is inferred that the increase in area of cultivation was the main factor which contributed to the increase in the growth rate of production.

Further analysis has revealed, that there was 39.93 per cent variation in the coconut production during the period of study. This variation was accompanied by wide variations in area by 32.91 per cent and productivity by 18.82 per cent. On an average, the volume of production of coconut in Tamil Nadu to that of India as a whole, was 26.78 per cent.

Production of Coconut in Kanyakumari District

It is found that in Kanyakumari District, the area under coconut cultivation which stood at 17284 hectares in 1986-87 has increased to 24220 hectares in 2005-06. It is found that the trend value for area under coconut cultivation in Kanyakumari District show an increase from 16968.59 hectares in 1986-87 to 23780.31 hectares in 2005-06. It is observed that production of coconut in Kanyakumari District had fluctuated from 1986-87 to 2005-06.

Analysis of production revealed that the trend value had marked an increase from 1786.40 lakhs nuts in 1986-89 to 3084.20 lakhs nuts in 2005-06. It is also observed that productivity of coconut in Kanyakumari District had been fluctuating during the period under review, with a gradual increase from 6995 nuts per hectare in 1986-87 to 8719 nuts per hectare in 1987-88. The trend value of productivity has also increased from 10353.14 in 1986-89 to 13352.36 in 2005-06.

Regarding the area of cultivation of coconut in the different Taluks of Kanyakumari District, Kalkulam taluk has been ranked first with an average area of 7902.05 hectares out of the total average area of 20374.7, contributing 38.78 per cent to the total area of coconut cultivation. The trend in area of coconut cultivation in Kalkulam taluk has increased remarkably from 6477 hectares in 1986-87 to 9383 hectares in 2005-06. Agasteeswaram taluk has been ranked second, with an average area of 6663.15 hectares out of the total average area of 20374.7, contributing 32.70 per cent to total area of coconut cultivation. The trend in area of coconut cultivation in the taluk, has shown an increasing trend from 5703 hectares in 1986-87 to 8048 hectares in 2005-06.

It is observed that Vilavancode taluk ranked third, contributing 22.34 per cent of the total area of coconut cultivation. The trend in area of coconut cultivation in the taluk has increased from 4099 hectares in 1986-87 to 5063 hectares in 2005-06 with some increase and decrease here and there. Thovalai taluk has been ranked the last, contributing 6.17 per cent of total area of coconut cultivation. The trend in area of coconut cultivation in the taluk, has increased continuously from 1005 hectares in 1986-87 to 1726 hectares in 2005-06.

Among the various taluks, Kalkulam taluk has been ranked first, with an annual average production of 949.9 lakhs nuts out of the overall average production of 2435.7 lakh nuts constituting 39.00 per cent of the total production of coconut. The trend in production of coconut in the taluk, has increased from 453 lakh nuts in 1986-87 to 1345 lakh nuts in 1999-200 and has reduced to 938 lakh nuts in 2005-06. Agasteeswaram taluk has been ranked second with an annual average production of 794.9 lakh nuts out of the overall annual average coconut production of 2435.7 lakh nuts, constituting 32.64 per cent of the overall average production of coconut. The trend in production of coconut in the taluk, has shown an increasing trend from 399 lakh nuts in 1986-87 to 804 lakh nuts in 2005-06.

It is found that Vilavancode taluk has ranked third, with an average production of 544.05 lakh coconuts out of the overall average production of 2435.7 lakh nuts constituting 22.34 per cent of the overall average production of coconut. The trend in production of coconut in the taluk has increased from 287 lakh nuts to 506 lakh nuts during the study period, with some gradual increase and decrease now and then. Thovalai taluk has been ranked the last with an annual average production of 146.85 lakh nuts out of the annual average production of 2435.7 lakh nuts, constituting 6.03 per cent of the overall average production of coconut. The trend in production of coconut in the taluk has increased with a little fluctuation from 70 lakh nuts in 1986-87 to 172 lakh nuts in 2005-06.

The productivity of coconut is found to vary in the different taluks of Kanyakumari District. Among the various taluks, Kalkulam taluk ranked first with an average productivity of 11890.1 nuts per hectare, out of the overall average productivity of 47190.45 nuts per hectare, constituting 25.20 per cent of the overall average productivity of coconut. The trend in productivity of coconut in the taluk has increased remarkably from 6994 nuts per hectare in 1986-87 to 15755 nuts per hectare in 1999-2000 and then with a gradual decrease from 14,872 to 9997 nuts per hectare in 2005-06. Vilavancode taluk ranked second with an average productivity of 11862.75 nuts per hectare out of the overall average coconut productivity of 47190.45 nuts per hectare, constituting 25.14 per cent of the overall average productivity of coconut. The trend in productivity of coconut in the taluk has shown an excellent increasing trend, from 7002 nuts per hectare in 1986-87 to 15760 nuts per hectare in 1999-2000 and the productivity decreased to 9994 nuts per hectare in 2005-06.

Analysis reveals that Agasteeswaram taluk ranked third, with an average productivity of 11843.9 nuts per hectare out of the overall average productivity of 47190.45 nuts per hectare, constituting 25.10 per cent of the overall average productivity of coconut. The trend in productivity of coconut in the taluk, has increased from 6996 nuts per hectare in 1986-87 to 15754 nuts per hectare in 1999-2000 and it started decreasing to reach the level of 9990 nuts per hectare in 2005-06. Thovalai taluk has been ranked the last, with an average productivity of 11593.7 nuts per hectare out of the total productivity of 47190.45 nuts per hectare constituting 24.57 per cent of productivity of coconut. The trend in productivity of coconut in the taluk has increased with some fluctuations from 6965 nuts per hectare in 1986-87 to 9965 nuts per hectare in 2005-06.

The average production of coconut all over India is 11438.1, 3115.6 in Tamil Nadu and 243.5 in Kanyakumari District.

The analysis on growth rate has revealed that the area under coconut cultivation, production and productivity in Agasteeswarm Taluk increased at the rate of 4.6 per cent per annum, 8.07 per cent per annum and 3.32 per cent per annum respectively. It is inferred that the increase in the area of cultivation and application of latest technologies were the main factors, which contributed to the increase in growth rate of production. Further, the analysis of co-efficient of variation revealed, that the taluk recorded 11.80 per cent variation in the area of coconut cultivation. For the same period, the rate of variation was 26.42 per cent in production and 21.34 per cent in productivity.

The analysis on growth rate revealed that area under coconut cultivation, production and productivity in Kalkulam Taluk increased at the rate of 5.15 per cent per annum, 8.92 per cent per annum and 3.59 per cent per annum respectively. Further, the analysis of co-efficient of variation revealed, that the taluk recorded 12.93 per cent variation in the area of coconut cultivation. For the same period, the rate of variation was 27.70 per cent in production and 20.89 per cent in productivity.

The analysis on growth rate revealed that area under coconut cultivation, production and productivity in Vilavancode Taluk increased at the rate of 1.37 per cent per annum, 5.07 per cent per annum and 3.55 per cent per annum respectively. Further the analysis of co-efficient of variation revealed that the taluk, recorded 5.99 per cent variation in the area of coconut cultivation. For the same period, the rate of variation was 23.94 per cent in production and 21.09 per cent in productivity.

The analysis on growth rate revealed that area under coconut cultivation, production and productivity in Thovalai

Taluk increased at the rate of 16.18 per cent per annum, 8.61 per cent per annum and 2.70 per cent per annum respectively. Further, the analysis of co efficient of variation revealed that the taluk recorded 16.18 per cent variation in the area of coconut cultivation. For the same period, the rate of variation was 27.49 per cent in production and 21.54 per cent in productivity.

The growth rate analysis revealed that area under coconut cultivation, production and productivity in Vilavancode increased at the rate of 4.15 per cent per annum, 7.78 per cent per annum and 3.48 per cent per annum respectively. Further the analysis of co efficient of variation revealed, that the taluk recorded 10.58 per cent variation in the area of coconut cultivation. For the same period, the rate of variation was 26.06 per cent in production and 21.13 per cent in productivity. In a nutshell, it is remarked that Vilavancode taluk is the least, with low variation and high growth rate in area of production and productivity.

Cost and Returns Analysis

The Cost and Returns analysis revealed that the total variable costs worked out to ₹ 62548.47, ₹ 57491.36 and ₹ 51345.88 respectively for marginal, small and large farmers, recording 49.19 per cent, 45.14 per cent and 41.30 per cent in the case of marginal farmers, small farmers and large farmers respectively. The contribution of fixed cost to the total establishment cost was ₹ 64603.35 (50.81%) for marginal farmers, ₹ 69867.25 (54.86%) for small farmers and ₹ 72992.50 (58.70%) for large farmers.

In the case of marginal farmers, of the total variable costs, human labour accounted for the maximum share of ₹ 34400.00 (27.05%) followed by cost of manure amounting to ₹ 14418.43 (11.34%). The interest on working capital borrowed for the purpose of cultivation, was estimated to be ₹ 9315.73 (7.33%) followed by cost of fertilizer amounting to ₹ 2660.32 (2.09%) and seedlings valued at ₹ 1003.84 (0.79%). Besides these factors, the cost of pesticides accounted for about ₹ 750.15 which amounted to 0.59 per cent of the total variable costs.

In the case of small farmers, of the total variable costs, human labour accounted for the maximum share of ₹ 32160.20 (25.25%) followed by cost of manure ₹ 12615.70 (9.91%). The interest on working capital, borrowed for the purpose of cultivation, was estimated to be ₹ 8562.54 (6.72%), followed by cost of fertilizer amounting to ₹ 2510.64 (1.97%) and seedlings valued at ₹ 926.50 (0.73%). Besides these factors, the cost of pesticides accounted for about ₹ 715.78 which was 0.56 per cent of the total variable costs.

In the case of large farmers, of the total variable costs, human labour accounted for the maximum share of ₹ 29898.25 (24.05%) followed by cost of manure amounting to ₹ 10129.29 (8.15%). The interest on working capital, borrowed for the purpose of cultivation, was estimated to be ₹ 7647.26 (6.15%) followed by cost of fertilizers being ₹ 2267.98 (1.82%) and seedlings amounting to ₹ 712.50 (57%). Besides these factors, the cost of pesticides accounted for about ₹ 690.60 which amounted to 0.56 per cent of the total variable costs.

Of all the variable costs human labour accounted for the maximum share in the case of all the three categories of farmers.

The total fixed costs worked out to ₹ 64603.35, ₹ 69867.25 and ₹ 72992.50 respectively for marginal farmers, small and large farmers. In other words, the total fixed cost accounted for 50.81 per cent, 54.86 per cent and 58.70 per cent in the case of marginal farmers, small farmers and large farmers respectively. The contribution of fixed cost to the net establishment cost was ₹ 11967.01 for marginal farmers, ₹ 116348.66 for small farmers and ₹ 108475.78 for large farmers.

In the case of marginal farmers, of the total fixed costs, rental value of land accounted for the maximum share of ₹ 45000 (35.39%) followed by other fixed costs amounting to ₹ 18853.35 (14.83%). Besides these factors, land revenue accounted for about ₹ 750.00 which was 0.59 per cent of the total fixed costs.

In the case of small farmers, of the total fixed costs, rental value of land accounted for the maximum share of ₹ 45000 (35.33%) followed by other fixed costs amounting to ₹ 24117.25 (18.94%). Besides these factors, land revenue accounted for about ₹ 750.00 constituting to 0.59 per cent of the total fixed costs.

In the case of large farmers, of the total fixed costs, rental value of land accounted for the maximum share of ₹ 45000 (36.19%) followed by other fixed costs amounting to ₹ 27242.50 (21.91%). Besides these factors, land revenue accounted for about ₹ 750.00 constituting 0.60 per cent of the total fixed costs.

Further analysis, regarding average total cost of coconut production, worked out to ₹ 32232.24 per acre in the case of marginal farmers, ₹ 31212.23 for small farmers and ₹ 30443.20 for large farmers. In other words the total cost of coconut production was the maximum, in the case of the marginal farmers, followed by small farmers and large farmers.

Thus it is found that, human labour accounted for the maximum share of operational and maintenance cost in all the three categories of farmers.

Cost analysis has revealed that the total fixed costs per acre worked out to ₹ 14516.35, ₹ 15524.77 and ₹ 16046.18 respectively in the case of marginal, small and large farmers. The proportion of total fixed cost by marginal farmers was 45.04 per cent marginal farmers, 49.74 per cent small farmers and 52.71 per cent large farmers. The contribution of fixed cost to the total cost of production was ₹ 32232.24 for marginal farmers, ₹ 31212.23 for small farmers and ₹ 30443.20 for large farmers.

The results of the analysis also indicated that the total cost of cultivation of coconut ranged from ₹ 32232.24 per acre in the case of marginal farmers to ₹ 30443.2 in the case of large farmers. The cost of production per nut was ₹ 4.62 for marginal farmers, 4.38 for small farmers and ₹ 3.94 for large farmers. Scientific method of cultivation adopted by large farmers must have been the main reason for the larger output and less cost of production.

The analysis of profitability, among the three categories of farmers revealed that the maximum profit of ₹ 29252.69, ₹ 24407.35 and ₹ 21177.16 respectively were realised in the case of large farmers, small farmers and marginal farmers. Similarly, the amount of fixed cost of production of coconut also ranged from ₹ 16046.18 in the case of large farmers to ₹ 14516.35 in the case of marginal farmers, whereas an amount of ₹ 15524.77 was contributed as fixed cost in the case of small farmers.

Further analysis revealed that the net profit ranged between ₹ 13206.51, the highest among large farmers, to ₹ 6660.81 the lowest among small farmers. The net profit ratio was the highest of 30.26 in the case of large farmers and the lowest of 17.13 in the case of marginal farmers and 22.15 in the case of small farmers. The analysis further revealed that the gross selling price and the net selling price were 5.70, 5.74 and 5.75 and 5.58, 5.63 and 5.65 respectively in the case of marginal farmers, small farmers and large farmers.

The cost and returns analysis revealed that cultivation of coconut was profitable. To ascertain the scope for further increase of net return per acre, resource-use-efficiency was analysed. Cobb Douglas type productive function was fitted, to evaluate resource productivity and returns to scale in coconut cultivation.

The relationship between yield of coconut and independent variables, during the yield stage, among marginal farmers revealed that the value of co-efficient of multiple determination (R^2) was 0.819, which indicated that 82 per cent of variation in the yield could be explained by the independent variables that are included in the function. The regression co-efficients are partial elasticities of production of coconut, with respect to the inputs concerned. The yield of coconut was significantly influenced by the level of the labour utilized.

The relationship between the yield and labour level indicated that one per cent increase in the level of labour used, keeping all other factors constant, would increase the yield by 0.389 per cent in its mean level. The coconut yield was also significantly influenced by the level of total cost of fertilizers and total cost of manure. The analysis indicated that every one per cent increase in the level of fertilizers applied ceteris paribus could increase the yield by 0.258 per cent from its mean level, while one per cent increase in the level of manures used ceteris paribus could increase the yield by 0.147 per cent from its mean level.

Further the analysis also indicated that relationship between cost of seedling and yield was positive, but not significant statistically. Therefore, the cost of seedling had no significant influence on the yield. The relationship between total number of coconut trees and yield was negative and statistically significant. It implies that one per cent increase in the number of trees would decrease the yield by 0.0657 per cent from its mean level.

In the case of small farmers it was found that the value of co-efficient of multiple determinations (R^2) was 0.873 which indicated that 87 per cent of variation in the yield could be explained by the independent variables that are included in the function. The regression co-efficients are partial elasticities of production of coconut with respect to the inputs concerned.

The yield of coconut was significantly influenced by the level of the labour utilized. One per cent increase in the level of labour used, keeping all other factors constant, would increase the yield by 0.241 per cent in its mean level.

The coconut yield was also significantly influenced by the cost of fertilizers and cost of manure. The analysis indicated that every one per cent increase in the level of fertilizer, applied ceteris paribus could increase the yield by 0.199 per cent from its mean level, while one per cent increase in the level of manures used ceteris paribus, could increase the yield by 0.295 per cent from its mean level.

The analysis also indicated that relationship between cost of seedling and yield was positive, but not significant statistically. Therefore, the cost of seedling had no significant influence on the yield. The relationship between the number of coconut trees and yield was negative and statistically significant. It implies that one per cent increase in the number of trees, would decrease the yield by 0.0972 from its mean level.

The analysis of estimated Cobb Douglas production function for large farmers revealed, that the value of co-efficient of multiple determinations (R^2) was 0.846 which indicated that 85 per cent of variation in the yield could be explained by the independent variables that are included in the function. The regression co-efficients are partial elasticities of production of coconut, with respect to the inputs concerned. The yield of coconut was significantly influenced by the level of labour utilized. One per cent increase in the level of labour used, keeping all other factors constant, would increase the yield by 0.89 from its mean level.

The coconut yield was also significantly influenced by the level of cost of fertilizer and cost of manure. The analysis indicated that every one per cent increase in the level of fertilizer applied, ceteris paribus, could increase the yield by 0.237 per cent from its mean level. While one per cent increase in the level of manures used ceteris paribus, could increase the yield by 0.143 per cent from its mean level. The analysis also indicated that the relationship between the cost of seedling and yield was positive, but not significant statistically. Therefore, the cost of seedling had no significant influence on the yield. The relationship between the total number of coconut trees and the yield was positive but statistically not significant. Therefore, the total number of coconut trees had no significant influence on the yield.

The analysis also revealed that the sum of elasticities for the yield increasing stage was 1.1483 for marginal farmers, 1.6028 for small farmers and 1.4704 for large farmers in coconut cultivation in the study area. It has been found that there is no farm which has less than unity of elasticity. On the other hand, the sum of elasticities was greater than unity in all categories. The results showed that there was increasing return to scale in all categories of farmers in the study region.

The analysis of resource-use-efficiency, in the case of yield increasing stage revealed, that the marginal physical products of labour, cost of manure and cost of fertilizers were 58.872, 0.306 and 1.714 respectively. The marginal value of inputs were also ₹ 328.50, ₹ 1.71 and ₹ 9.56 respectively. It was found that there is scope for the increasing the use of labour, fertilizers and manures to increase the yield of coconut further, in the case of marginal farmers as the ratio of marginal value product to factor cost was more than unity. It also revealed that every rupee additionally spent on those variables, would increase the value of yield further by ₹ 1.53, ₹ 1.71 and ₹ 9.56 respectively.

The analysis also indicated that the marginal physical products of labour, cost of manure and cost of fertilizers were 41,470, 0.725 and 1.523 respectively. The marginal values of inputs were also ₹ 233.48, ₹ 4.08 and ₹ 8.57 respectively. It is inferred from Table 5.10 that there was scope for increasing the use of labour, fertilizers and manures to increase the yield of coconut further in the case of small farmers as the ratio of marginal value product to factor cost was more than unity. It also revealed that every rupee additionally spent on those variables, would increase the value of yield further by ₹ 1.09, ₹ 4.08 and ₹ 8.57 respectively.

It was found that the marginal physical products of labour, cost of manure and cost of fertilizers were 17.891, 0.356 and 1.935 respectively. The marginal value of inputs were also ₹ 101.09, ₹ 2.01 and ₹ 10.93 respectively. It is inferred from the table 5.11 that there was scope for increasing the use of labour, fertilizers and manures to increase the yield of coconut further in the case of large farmers as the ratio of marginal value product to factor cost was more than unity except labour. It also revealed that every rupee additionally spent on those variables, would increase the value of yield further by ₹ 0.47, ₹ 2.01 and ₹ 10.93 respectively. Thus it can be concluded that the analysis indicated that there was a scope for increasing the coconut yield by better utilization of these variables.

Capital productivity analysis of different market prices indicated that the pay-back period of coconut cultivation was 10.43 years in the case of marginal farmers, followed by 9.75 years in the case of the small farmers and only 8.19 years in the case of large farmers. The pay back period has been less than 10 years in all the categories of farmers except the marginal. As the pay back period is less than the cut-off period in the case of small and large farmers, it can be concluded that coconut cultivation is viable. It is also viable in marginal farmers as the difference is very meagre.

The net present value was estimated to be ₹ 36329.94 at 10 per cent discount rate, in the case of marginal farmers, followed by ₹ 61511.31 in the case of small farmers and the highest of ₹ 95988.79 in the case of large farmers. Since the net present value is positive and large, it is inferred that the capacity to generate more wealth is large in coconut farms. Therefore, the investment in coconut cultivation is economically beneficial.

The computed value of Internal Rate of Return of Coconut cultivation was 14.88 per cent for the marginal farmers followed by 16.60 per cent for the small farmers and 18.96 for the large farmers. As compared to the opportunity cost of capital (cut off rate) which was taken as 10 per cent, the rate of return on investment made in coconut cultivation is high. It indicates that there is economic viability of investment in coconut cultivation.

Marketing of Coconut

The different marketing channels identified in the marketing of coconut in the study area were :

Channel I: Producer—Village trader—Wholesaler—Retailer—Consumer

Channel II : Producer—Wholesaler—Retailer—Consumer

Channel III: Producer—Village trader—Retailer—Consumer

In the study area, it is observed that the percentage of marketable surplus to the total quantity of coconut produced among the marginal farmers, worked out to 99.15 per cent while for the small farmers it worked out to 99.21 per cent and it was worked out to 99.38 per cent among the large farmers. Further, the analysis revealed that all categories of farmers retained only less than one per cent of their coconut production for meeting their family and other requirements.

The analysis of storing habits among the growers revealed that the sample marginal farmers stored 23.50 per cent of the marketable surplus anticipating remunerative prices. It was 36.78 per cent in the case of sample small farmers and 23.50 per cent in sample large farmers. The percentage of storage loss to the quantity of coconut stored worked out to 0.99 per cent, 0.85 per cent and 0.71 per cent, in the case of marginal, medium and large farmers respectively which was less than one per cent of the quantity stored.

It is also observed that the percentage of marketed surplus to the marketable surplus worked out to 99.77 per cent in the case of marginal farmers, where as it was 99.69 per cent in the case of small farmers and 99.61 per cent in the case of large farmers. The marginal farmers sold 79.23 per cent of their produce and small farmers 71.28 per cent and the large farmers sold only 58.00 per cent of their produce to village traders.

Price spread analysis showed that the cost incurred by the producer in marketing one thousand coconuts worked out to ₹90 in Channel I and ₹130 in Channel II, with an overall average of ₹110 per thousand coconuts. The comparative analysis revealed that the commission/brokerage incurred by the producer in marketing coconut was the maximum, when the average is taken into account. This cost was followed by tax and village mahamai and transportation cost, which were more in Channel I, and loading and unloading expenses were the least in both the Channels but comparatively high in Channel II.

The analysis of cost incurred by the village traders in marketing coconuts was ₹373 per thousand coconuts, whereas it was ₹430 per thousand coconuts and ₹191 per thousand coconuts in the case of wholesalers and retailers respectively. The producer's share in the price paid by the consumer is estimated to be around 81 per cent in all the three channels in the study area.

It was found that the marketing cost incurred by the producer was lower in Channel I and III compared to Channel II, because of the absence of commission charges in the former.

Price-spread analysis showed that both, Channel I and III are best from the producer's point of view. However, the producer prefers retailers. Between Channels I and II, Channel II is more profitable to the producer.

It was observed from the study, that the price-spread in Channel II is the lowest with ₹1194 per 1000 nuts because of less marketing cost and higher producer's price. The producer's price was the maximum in Channel II with ₹5770 per 1000 coconuts followed by ₹5470 per 1000 coconuts in Channels I and II. The price-spread in Channel I was the highest among all the channels because of the existence of more number of marketing intermediaries and more marketing cost.

Among the three channels, Channel III seems to be the most efficient. The efficiency index for Channel III is the maximum with 9.65, followed by Channel II with 8.27. The marketing efficiency in Channel III is better than that in the remaining two channels because of less marketing cost.

In the marketing area, it had been identified that most of the farmers face many problems relating to the cultivation of coconut in their farms. These include incidence of pests and diseases, High cost of input, Lack of irrigation, Shortage of tree climbers and Lack of scientific knowledge.

The analysis of the most crucial problems faced by sample growers in cultivation of coconut, with the help of Garette ranking technique showed that the incidence of pests and diseases was the major problem in coconut cultivation by village farmers which ranked first, with a mean score of 56.36. Lack of scientific knowledge among the cultivators ranked the last with the least mean score of 39.92.

The various problems faced by the growers, in marketing of coconut include 'Price fluctuation', 'Absence of Cooperative society', 'Lack of Market Information', 'Inadequate Storage Facility' and 'Exploitation by Middlemen'. Further analysis revealed that 'Price Fluctuation' is the major problem faced by the growers with a mean score of 55.09. 'Exploitation by Middlemen' is found to be the least important problem faced by the growers in the study area, with the lowest mean score of 37.17.

The price of coconut always depends on the national and international demand and supply position. The analysis also showed that there has been a significant increase in the price of coconut over the years. During the study period the annual average price of coconut per quintal, has increased at the rate of ₹92.04 per annum. The result of cyclical variation indicated that there were recurrent up and down movements around secular trend levels. The indices of irregular variations for the price of coconut in the Kannyakumari market, ranged from 0.76 to 1.31. The co-efficient of variation of irregular variation is 16.53 per cent. It could be observed form the seasonal indices, that the lower prices prevailed from April to October and January to March.

Suggestions

Improved and hybrid varieties of coconuts, which are pest-resistant and drought-tolerant should be supplied to the small, medium and large farmers, through the coconut farms or nurseries owned by the Government, at a subsidised rate or even free of cost. In order to develop drought and pest resistant coconut varieties, the latest bio-technologies like Genetic engineering, Tissue culture and Vermi culture may be applied which will achieve the maximum level of productivity.

The scientific methods of coconut cultivation must be made known to the growers of coconut very often by the Government organizations and extension agencies, using all popular media of communication.

Insurance for coconut plantations may be introduced to make good the loss incurred by the growers, when the plantations become a victim to natural calamities like the Tsunami. This will go a long way in saving the coconut industry.

Of late, due to global warming and factors like EL-nino and La-nina phenomena, the monsoon patterns seem to be erratic, which tells upon the productivity of coconut. Therefore, to ensure consistently good yield, various irrigation methods like pump irrigation and drip irrigation, may be followed and the Government can grant subsidy or interest-free loans in this regard.

Cooperative farming may be taken up by enclosing large areas for cultivation. In such a case, integrated pest management, effective labour management and coordinated functioning in all aspects of cultivation are possible.

Grading and processing facilities may be provided at the production centres so that the coconut growers would get the right price for their produce. Information on marketing should be passed on to the cultivators and traders through the mass media and other means of communication.

Establishment of warehouses at the production centres must be done and this must be maintained by the local governments at minimum charges to the growers.

Value-added products must be popularized in domestic markets through organized marketing network. New industries may be started to manufacture value-added products and new systems of marketing may be introduced to sell them at standard prices.

Conclusion

As coconut is also a significant foreign exchange earner and a source of income and employment to millions of people this study has been undertaken. Another aim is, mainly, to help the Government to take up policy decisions and formulate suitable schemes and programmes to ameliorate socio-economic conditions of the coconut cultivators. The present study has brought into focus, various issues relating to production and marketing of coconut. The policy implications suggested, if properly implemented, may result in increased revenue for the nation and the people concerned. Based on the experience of the researcher, the following issues have been identified for further research:

(*i*) Economics of Coconut Cultivation—A Cost Effect Analysis (*ii*) Production and Marketing of Coconut in Kaniyakumari and Coimbatore districts—A Comparative Analysis

(*iii*) Economics of Coconut By-products—A Cost Effect Analysis

(*iv*) Coconut Cultivation in Two taluks of a District—A Study.

(*v*) Socio-economic conditions of Coconut farmers in Kanyakumari District—A Study.

The researcher will feel amply rewarded, if the present study paves the way for the above and many more similar studies in future and those studies will definitely contribute a lot to improve the well-being of the coconut growers in the country.

Bibliography

BOOKS

1. Agrawal N.K. (1992) *'Cost Accounting for C.A. Intermediate'*, Global Business Press, New Delhi.
2. Alpha.C.Chiang (1967) *'Fundamental Methods of Mathematical Economics'*, Mc Graw-hill Kogakusha Ltd., Tokyo.
3. Aravindakshan M. (1995) *'Coconut Situation in India'*, Coconut Development Board, Kochi.
4. Child R. (1974) *'Coconuts'*, Longman Group Ltd., London.
5. Francis Cherunilam (2003), *'International Marketing Including Export Management'*, 6th Edition, Himalaya Publishing House, Mumbai.
6. Gupta S.P. (1991) *'Statistical Methods'*, Sultan Chand & Sons, New Delhi.
7. King. (2001) *'Economic Environment of Business'*, King Books, Nai. Sarak, Delhi.
8. Kothari C.R. (1996) *'Research Methodology'* Wishwa prakashan, New Delhi.
9. Markose V.T. (1994) *'Processing and Marketing of Coconuts in India'*, Coconut Development Board, Kochi.
10. Markose V.T. (1998) *'Coconut Development Board Activities and Achievements'*, Coconut Development Board, Kochi.
11. Markose V.T. (1998) *'The Coconut Palm—A Monograph'*, Indian Central Coconut Committee, Ernakulam.
12. Misra S.K. and Puri V.K. (2002) *'Indian Economy'*, 10th Edition, Himalaya Publishing House, Mumbai.
13. Richard l. Levin and David S. Rubin (1991) *'Statistics for Management'*, Prentice-Hall of India Private Ltd., New Delhi.

14. Singh H.P. & et. al. (1999) *'30 years of Coconut Industry'*, Coconut Development Board. Kochi.
15. Thamban P.K. (1990) *'Coconut Industry in India'*, Asian and Pacific Coconut, CDB, Ministry of Agriculture.
16. Thampan P.K. (1982) *'Handbook on Coconut Palm'* Oxford & IBH Publishing Co., New Delhi.
17. Thampan P.K. (1988) *'Glimpses of Coconut industry in India'*, Coconut Development Board, Kochi.

JOURNALS

1. Choudhury. D. (2002) 'Problems and Prospects of Coconut Cultivation in Assam', *Indian Coconut Journal*, Vol.XXXII, No.10, February.
2. Christopher Lourduraj A. and Mylswamy V. (1997) 'Coconut to Increase Productivity', *Kisan World*, Vol. 24, No.1 January.
3. Ganesa Moorthy K. Narayanan C. Packiaraj P. Rajarathinam S. and Khan H.H. (2003) 'Genetic Improvement in Coconut in Tamilnadu', *Indian Coconut Journal*, Volume XXIV, No.1, May.
4. Ganesan K.P. (2001) 'Coconut Farming—An Innovative Approach', *Kisan World*, Vol.28, No.8, August.
5. George V Thomas, Krishnakumar V. Dhanapal R. Murali Gopal and Alka Gupta (2006) 'Production Technology for Sustainable Coconut Cultivation', *Indian Coconut Journal*, Vol. XXXVII, No.2, June.
6. Gopulan K. and Venkiteraman, M.S. (1951) 'Cost of Cultivation of Coconut in Travancore', *Indian Coconut Journal*.
7. Hali R. (1996) 'New Horizons in Coconut Productivity', *Kisan World*, Vol. 23, No. 3 March.
8. Iyer R.P. et-al (1979) *'Super Yielder in Coconut'*, Indian Farming.
9. Jose Mahew (2003) 'Drip Irrigation—A Successful Technology with Multiple Benefits', *Kisan World*, Vol. 30, No. 1, January.
10. Kameswara Rao P. (1995) 'Coconut Marketing in Andhra Pradesh: Problems and Prospects', *Indian Coconut Journal*, Vol. XXVI, No.1 & 2, May & June.

11. Kaul G.L. (1995) 'Global Competitiveness of Coconut Industry,' *Indian Coconut Journal*, Vol. XXVI, No.4, August.

12. Lathika and Ajithkumar C.E. (2005) 'Growth Trends in Area, Production and Productivity of Coconut in India', *Indian Journal of Agricultural Economics*, Vol.60, No.4, October – December.

13. Maheshwari P.C. Rathika R. Edwin Ganadhas M. (2003) 'Marketing Strategies for Coconut', *Indian Journal of Marketing*, Vol. XXXIII, No.3, March.

14. Mohan Rajesh (2006) 'Increased Income from Coconut Plantation', *Kisan World*, Vol.33, No.7, July.

15. Nagarajan S.S. (1998) 'Improving Coconut Farm Productivity with Silt', *Kisan World*, Vol.25, No.5, May.

16. Nair M.K. and Rajesh M.K. (2001) 'Coconut Production and Productivity', *Indian Coconut Journal*, Vol.XXXIII, No.2, June.

17. Nair M.K. et.al. (1995) 'Competitiveness Through Cost Reduction and Higher Productivity in Coconut', *Indian Coconut Journal*, Vol. XXVI, No.4, August.

18. Namasivayam N. & Richard Paul V. (2006) 'Price Spread in Marketing of Coconut in Tamil Nadu' *Indian Journal of Marketing*, Vol. XXXVI, No.7, July 5.

19. Natarajan, C. Giridharan S. and Bhaskaran R. (2001) 'VHC 3-New Coconut Hybrid for Tamilnadu', *Indian Coconut Journal*, Vol.XXX1, No.9, January.

20. Pandalai M. (1999) 'Is Coconut Tract Bound?', *Indian Coconut Journal*, Vol. XXX, No.1, May.

21. Parameswara Gupta E.A. (1996) 'Trend in Area, Production and Productivity of Coconut in India. A Study of Karnataka', *Southern Economist*, Vol.35, No.15&16, December 1-15.

22. Parameswara Gupta E.A. (1997) 'Processing and Consumption of Coconut in India', *Southern Economist*, Vol.35, No 19, February 1.

23. Punchideva P.G. (2000) 'Current Status of the Coconut Industry', *Indian Coconut Journal*, Vol. XXXI, No.6, October.

24. Rajkumar S. and Thamilselvan R. (2005) 'Importance of Coconut Cultivation', *Kisan World*, Vol.32, No.5, May.

25. Sivanappan R.K. (2004) 'Drip Irrigation for Coconut for Increased Yield', *Kisan World*, Vol. 31, No. 10, October.
26. Sreekumar Poduval, (1995) 'Technologies for Non-traditional Coconut Products', *Indian Coconut Journal*, May and June.
27. Sugata Ghose (1993) 'Coconut Production—A New Look', *Kisan World*, Vol.20, No.11, November.
28. Sugata Ghose (1998) 'Coconut-India's Pride', *Kisan World*, Vol.25, No.8, August.
29. Sugata Ghose. (2000) 'Progress in Coconut', *Kisan World*, Vol.27, No.5, May.
30. Surendirakumar P.S. Kalyanasundaram D. Kavitha S. and Sampathkumar G. (2005) 'Inter Cropping in Coconut to Improve the Farm Productivity', *Indian Coconut Journal*, Vol. XXXIII, No.5, September.
31. Thampan P.K. (1999) 'Profitability of Coconut Farming', *Kisan World*, Vol.26, No.10, October.
32. Veerputhiran R. (2005) 'Drip Irrigation for Sustainable Water Management', *Kisan World*, Vol. 32, No. 1, January.
33. Venkitaswamy R. and Hameed Khan H. (2004) 'Drought Management in coconut in Tamil Nadu', *Indian Coconut Journal*, Vol. XXX1V, No.10. February.

REPORTS

1. *4th Annual Report, Kanyakumari Central Co-operative Bank Ltd*, 2002-2003, pp. 8-9.
2. *Action Plan* 1997-1998 to 2001-2002, district Industries Centre. Konam.
3. *Administrative Report of Kanyakumari Market Committee*. Kanyakumari District.
4. *AGROSTAT*, Joint Director of Agriculture, Kanyakumari District, 2003, p.126.
5. *AGROSTAT*, Joint Director of Agriculture, Kanyakumari, 2003, p.2.
6. Annual Report (1998) *'Coconut Cultivation'*, Coconut Development Board, Tamilnadu.
7. *Annual Report of the Department of Statistics*, Government of India, Nagercoil.

8. *Annual Report of the Directorate of Economics and Statistics*, Ministry of Agriculture, Government of India, Chennai.
9. *Annual Report of the Joint Director*, Department of Agriculture, Nagercoil.
10. Census of India, *Kanyakumari District Census Hand Book*, Parts XIII, A and B, 1981.
11. Census of India, *Madras District Census Hand Book*, Kanyakumari, 1981.
12. *Credit Palm for Kanyakumari District*, Lead Cell, I.O.B, 1988-1990.
13. *Gazetteers of India*, Kanyakumari District, 1995.
14. Nair P.K. (1976) *'Intensive Cropping for Stabilized Income at Enhanced Rates from Coconut Plantation'* Financing Agriculture.
15. *Season and Crop Report of Tamilnadu*, 1998-99.
16. *Statistical Hand Book of Tamil Nadu*, 1985.

THESES

1. Chandran (1992). *'A Study of Coconut Marketing in Tamil Nadu'*, Ph.D thesis submitted to Madurai Kamaraj University, Madurai.
2. Mark Linson (1982) *'Marketing of Coconuts in Agasteeswaram Taluk of Kanyakumari Districts'*. Unpublished M.Phil Dissertation submitted to Madurai Kamaraj University.

NEWSPAPERS

1. Markose V.T. (2000) 'Coconut-assured Bright Future', *The Hindu Survey of Indian Agriculture.*
2. Prabhu M. J. 'Increasing Coconut Yield in Coastal Sand and Soils', Farmers Note Book-*The Hindu*, March 30.
3. Rajagopal V. ArulRaj S. Sairam C. V. (2004) 'Coconut Industry—Improving Genetic Produce' *The Hindu Survey of Indian Agriculture.*
4. Rethinam P. (2004). 'Coconut—Making Industry Competitive', *The Hindu Survey of Indian Agriculture.*
5. Rethinam S. (2005) 'Coconut—Steps for Yield Increase', *The Hindu Survey of Indian Agriculture.*

WEBSITES

1. http://www.coconutboard.nic.in/tendnutr.htmtender coconut water.
2. Internet:http//www.fao.org/DOCREP/005/Y3612E/Y3612e03htm-p.1.
3. www.india.agronet.com
4. www.coconutboard.nic.in
5. www.fao.org
6. www.goggle.com
7. www.tn.gov.in.com

Index

B

C

D

E

G

I